Michael Busselle's Guide to

TRAVEL

& VACATION

PHOTOGRAPHY

RotoVision

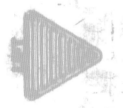

A RotoVision Book
Published and Distributed by RotoVision SA
Route Suisse 9
1295 Mies
Switzerland

RotoVision SA, Sales, Editorial & Production Office
Sheridan House, 112/116A Western Road
Hove BN3 1DD, England

Tel: +44 (0) 1273 72 72 68
Fax: +44 (0) 1273 72 72 69

ISBN 2-88046-721-7

Book design by Brenda Dermody
Cover design by Design Revolution

Production and separations in Singapore by ProVision Pte. Ltd.
Printed in China by Midas Printing

Michael Busselle's Guide to

TRAVEL

& VACATION

PHOTOGRAPHY

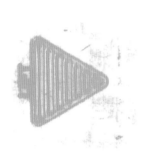

Contents

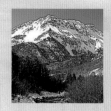

Destinations

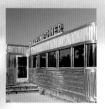

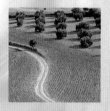

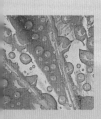

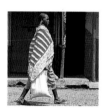

I

You are bound to have favourite subjects for photography,
but it's important to shoot a range of different themes so
you can capture a good all-round impression of the place you have visited. Taking pictures
from each of the groups listed in this chapter will ensure you will return with a selection which
encapsulates the character and
atmosphere of the place.

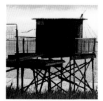

Of all the travel and landscape subjects, a beautiful view is probably the most commonly photographed. It is also, paradoxically, one of the most difficult from which to produce a striking image. The prime reason is that there is often a temptation to include too much in the frame which can result in an image which has no immediate focus of attention and too many conflicting details.

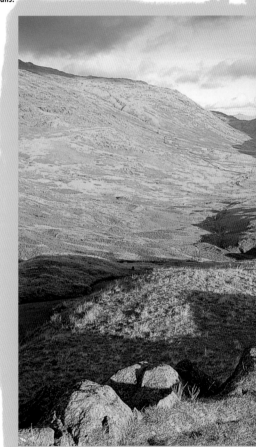

Seeing

It was the broad expanse of this Cumbrian scene which appealed to me combined with the rich autumnal colours. The clarity of the late afternoon sunlight was ideal for shooting a distant view and the strong shadows it created also enhanced the texture and contours of the landscape.

Thinking

I wanted to convey a strong impression of depth and distance within the scene using the foreground rocks to accentuate. The small highlighted cottage in the valley and the V shape in the horizon created a focus of attention for the composition.

location
Hardknott Pass - Cumbria UK

Technical Details
6x4.5cm Single Lens Reflex -
55mm lens, polarising,
81C warm-up and neutral-
graduated filters,
1/2 sec @ f22, Fuji Velvia.

Rule of Thumb

When both close and distant details are included in the image set a small aperture to ensure adequate depth of field and focus at a point about a third of the way between the nearest and furthest details.

location
Near Consuegra - La Mancha, Spain
This scene was shot in the softer light of a hazy summer day. I used a long-focus lens to isolate a small area of the scene and maximise the colour and pattern within the landscape.

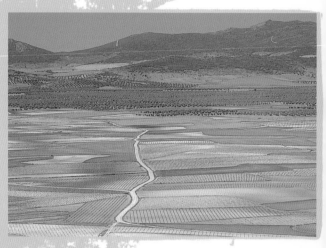

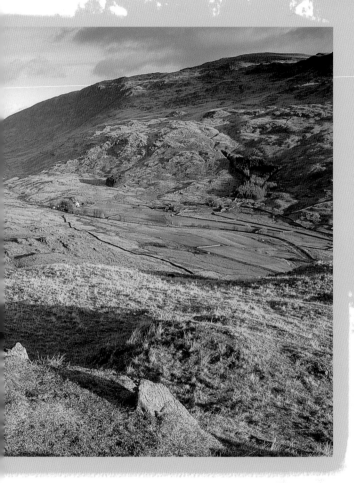

Technical Details
35mm Single Lens Reflex -
200mm lens, polarising,
81C warm-up, and neutral-
graduated filters,
Fuji Velvia.

Acting
I chose a viewpoint which enabled the rocks to almost fill the foreground and used a **wide-angle lens** to include as much of the scene as possible. I used a warm-up filter and polariser to emphasise the rich autumn colours.

Seeing

The contrast between the grey, wintry snow-capped mountain and the fresh spring-like green grass lit by a pool of sunlight was the inspiration for this shot.

Thinking

I wanted to accentuate the contrast between these two elements and keep the composition as a simple division of layers, one third mountain and two thirds grass.

Technical Details ➤
6x4.5cm Single Lens Reflex - 105mm lens neutral-graduated and 81C warm-up filters Fuji Velvia.

location
Puy de Sancy, near le Mont Dore - Auvergne, France

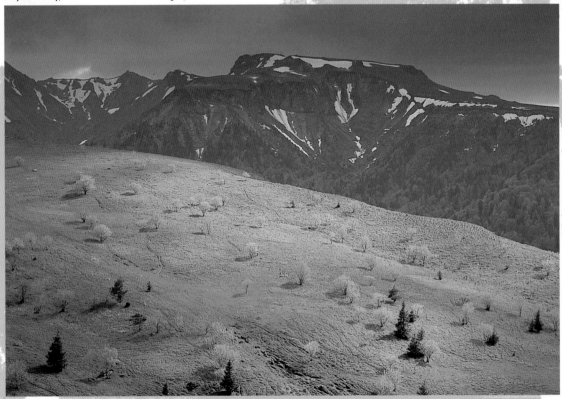

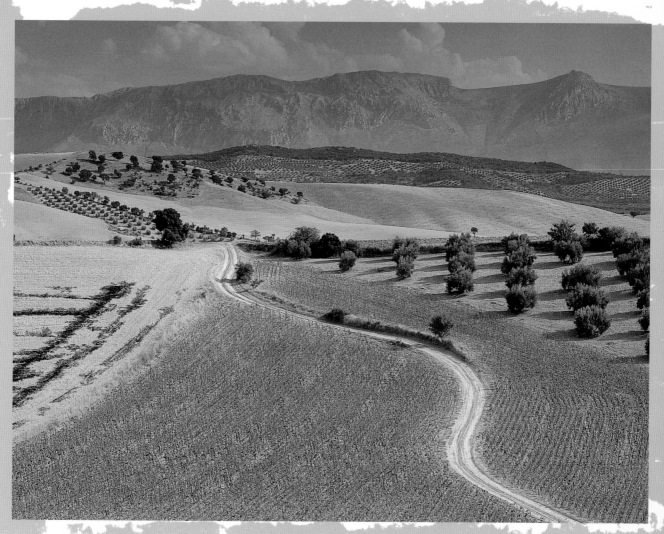

Technical Details
35mm Single Lens Reflex - 150mm lens neutral-graduated and 81C warm-up filters Fuji Velvia.

location
Sierra Magina, near Ubeda - Jaen, Spain
When the sky in a landscape photograph is weak or uninteresting it is best to include only a little of it or to exclude it altogether. It can also help to use a neutral graduated filter to make it darker.

Acting

I used a long-focus lens to isolate the most effective section of the scene, a neutral-graduated filter to make the mountainside as dark grey as possible and an 81C warm-up filter to enhance the colour of the grass.

Photographing Views

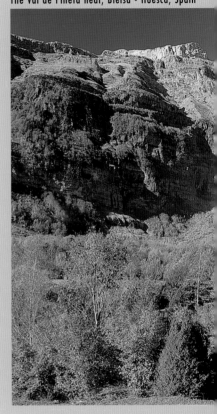

Seeing

The distant snow-capped mountain creating a backdrop to the fast running river was the aspect of this scene which made me want to shoot it.

Thinking

I felt that to accentuate the impression of depth and distance would add impact to the image and that the subject needed to be framed as an upright.

Acting

I found the most effective viewpoint was from the river bed with the water flowing directly towards the camera. I used a wide-angle lens to exaggerate the perspective and to include as much foreground as possible. I used a small aperture to obtain maximum depth of field and a polarising filter to increase the colour saturation and to give the snow more definition against the blue sky.

Technical Details
6x4.5cm Single Lens Reflex - 50mm lens, polariser and 81C warm-up filters, Fuji Velvia.

Technical Details
6x4.5cm Single Lens Reflex - 55mm lens, polarising and 81C warm-up filters, Fuji Velvia.

Rule of Thumb

With landscape photographs in particular it's often an automatic choice to frame them as horizontal images but quite often a composition can be more effective as an upright image and it's a good idea to always consider this option first.

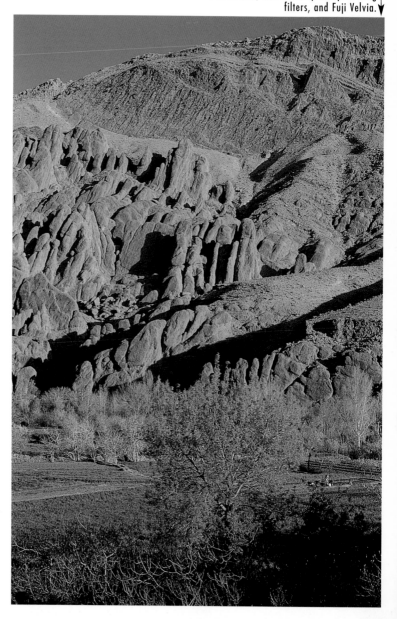

I used a long-focus lens for this picture of the Dades Gorge in Morocco, not because the light was not sharp enough for a wider view, but because the sun was low in the sky and the foreground was in deep shadow. I also wanted to frame the image tightly in order to exclude some distracting details each side of the area I photographed.

Technical Details
35mm SLR Camera with a 70–200mm zoom lens, 81B warm-up and polarising filters, and Fuji Velvia.

Acting

The road runs close to the beach here and I walked back along it until I found this tall pine tree. From this viewpoint, I was able also to see clear to the horizon and the wide-angle lens allowed me to include all of the small headland which juts out as well as part of the pine tree. As these elements are of a darker tone than the beach, it has resulted in the latter becoming very dominant in the image and the contrast has made all of the other colours seem richer. The illustration shows how the image would have been less striking, and had less feeling of depth, if the foreground tree had not been included.

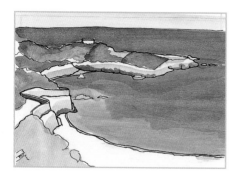

Technical Details
Medium-format SLR Camera with a 50mm wide-angle lens, 81C warm-up and polarising filters, and Fuji Velvia.

Rule of Thumb

You will stand a much better chance of shooting open views successfully if you plan to do it early or late in the day. At these times, the sun is at a low angle revealing stronger textures and there is less likelihood of atmospheric haze.

Seeing

A period of prolonged and heavy winter rain a couple of years ago brought an end to near-drought conditions in Spain's Andalucia, and the following spring released an astonishing display of wild flowers and lush foliage. This golden-coloured plant was covering vast tracts of the landscape to the east of Malaga and I searched avidly for a photogenic corner.

Thinking

Although sunny, it was a bit hazy and it was also in the middle of the day which meant the shadows were small and not very well defined, resulting in a slightly soft image with not quite enough bite, especially for an open view.

Technical Details Medium-format SLR Camera with a 50mm wide-angle lens, 81C warm-up and polarising filters, and Fuji Velvia.

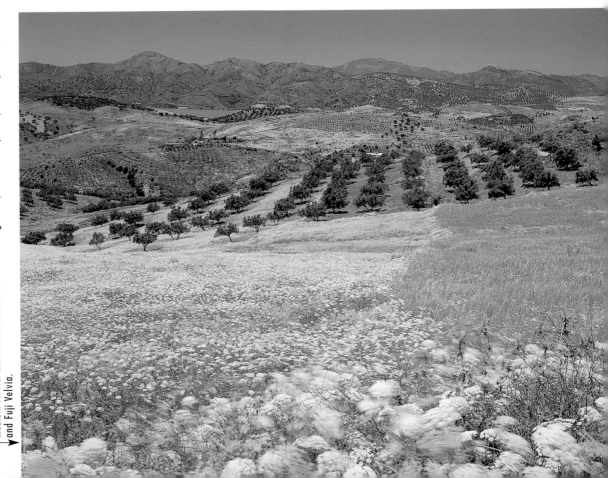

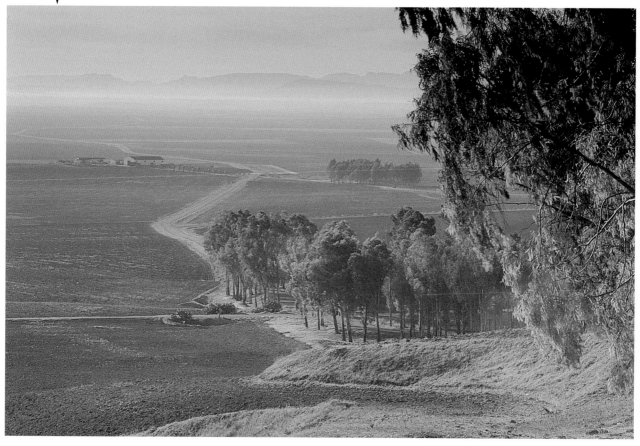

This view of the River Guadalquivir plain in Andalucia was taken on a similarly soft and hazy day, but was photographed quite early in the morning when the shadows were quite large. In this case the haze has contributed to the atmosphere of the picture, but it needed the inclusion of the shaded trees to prevent the image becoming flat and muddy.

Acting

I found this viewpoint up on a hillside looking down towards the Lake of Vinuela, and from here there was a quite breathtaking panorama which was dominated by the pale gold blooms. I set up my camera in a spot which enabled me to include some of the very light blooms which were close to the camera to raise the contrast of the image, as well as help emphasise the feeling of depth and distance. I framed the image to include the olive grove on the right as the red soil and dark green trees also added a degree of contrast. I fitted a polarising filter to increase the colour saturation and a warm-up filter to further enhance the gold colour.

Rule of Thumb

Unless the sun is really bright and strong and the atmosphere free from haze, there is always the likelihood that there will not be enough contrast for a really strong image when shooting summer landscapes, especially open views. Including foreground interest which creates a strong colour or tonal contrast with the rest of the scene is often an effective way of overcoming this.

Photographing Views

Seeing

The ancient perched village of Chateau Chalon, in France's Jura region, can be seen from a long way off. The vineyards which surround the village had turned to a vivid rust and ochre and I spent some time shooting pictures from a viewpoint below the village before driving up to see how things looked from there. It was early on an Autumn morning and the light was sharp and clear and, although I lost the benefit of the rich-coloured vineyards, the texture of the village houses and distant landscape more than compensated.

Thinking

My main concern was to include as much of the village as possible but also to show as large an area of the distant view as possible. However, the lower section of the landscape was still in shadow and I decided to wait a little until the sun rose high enough to light it more fully.

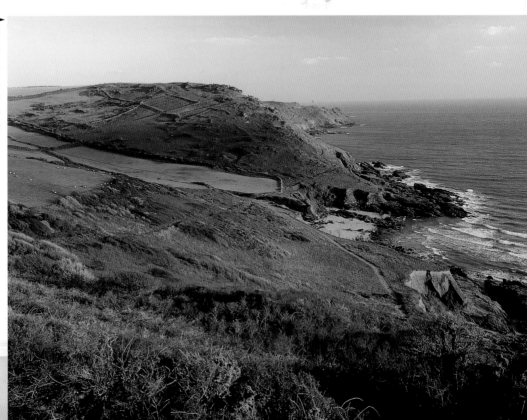

▲ Technical Details
35mm SLR Camera with a 70–200mm zoom lens, 81B warm-up and polarising filters, and Fuji Velvia.

Acting

I chose this **viewpoint** as it provided a good view of the village and an acceptable amount of the landscape beyond. I framed the image initially as a **landscape shape** as this included more of the view but when I tried it as an **upright** I felt that, although less was shown, it created a more compact and **balanced** composition.

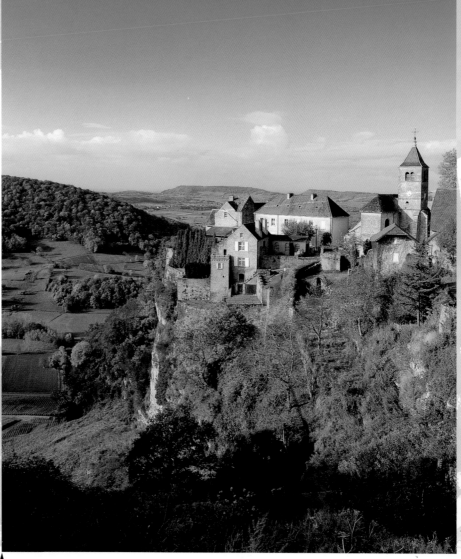

Technical Details

Medium-format SLR Camera with a 50mm wide-angle lens, 81A warm-up and polarising filters, and Fuji Velvia.

Gara Rock in the South Hams region of Devon in the UK was the location of this picture. It was taken late afternoon on a winter's day when the warm-tinted sunlight emphasised the rich red colour of the dead bracken. I chose a viewpoint which showed a good stretch of the coastline, using a wide-angle lens, and framed the image to include enough of the bracken-covered hillsides to balance the composition.

Rule of Thumb

Photographs are often taken in the landscape format when an upright framing would create a better composition. This is partly because it is easier and more comfortable to hold most cameras in the horizontal position. It can be helpful to adopt the habit of always looking first at the upright possibilities when initially framing a shot and in this way you won't overlook the chance of a stronger image.

Rivers & Waterfalls

From dark and mysterious to pale turquoise, crystal clear, rushing, motionless, sparkling and turgid, water has a constantly changing appearance which offers considerable photographic potential.

location
Lac du Der - Champagne Ardenne, France

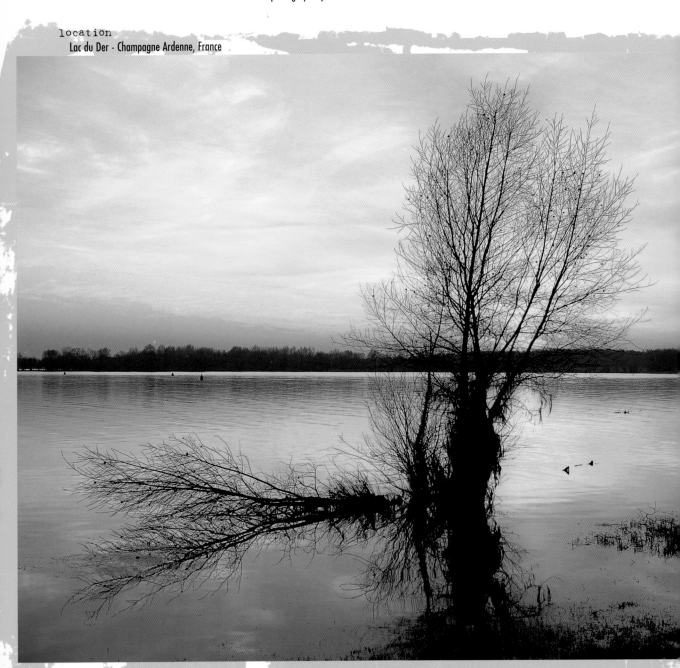

Seeing

The very still water of this lake created a mirror-like **reflection** of both the sky and the submerged tree and it was this, combined with the rich colours of the **sunset**, which appealed to me.

Thinking

I wanted to place the sun partially behind the tree to create a bold **focus of attention** and also to reduce its intensity. Because I wanted to emphasise the mirror effect I placed the horizon in the centre of the frame to divide the image into two equal halves.

Acting

I chose a viewpoint close to the lake shore so the **reflection** continued right into the **foreground** and used a wide-angle lens to include the full extent of the tree and its fallen branch, framing the shot so it created an L-shape along lines dividing the image into **thirds**.

Technical Details
6x4.5cm Single Lens Reflex - 55mm lens, Fuji Velvia.

Technical Details
6x4.5cm Single Lens Reflex - 55mm lens - neutral-graduated filter Fuji Velvia.

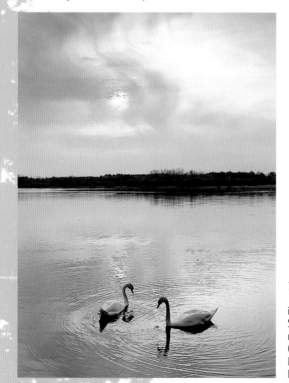

```
Rule of Thumb
```

When shooting pictures like sunsets and at dusk when the colours are very subtle, it's best to avoid the use of coloured filters, such as warm-ups. These can sometimes override the natural colour of the scene and create a rather artificial quality.

location
A lake in the Sologne, near Orleans, Loire, France

Rivers & Waterfalls

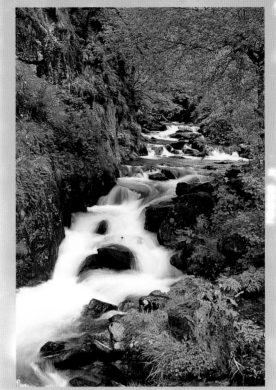

location
The Val 'Aran, near Viella - Lerida, Spain

Seeing

The canopy of fresh green foliage enclosing the small stream suggested the potential of this shot and the soft lighting and limited colour range contributed to the tranquil atmosphere.

Thinking

I wanted to emphasise the secretive quality of the scene and make the most of the water so I decided to frame the image quite tightly and use a slow shutter speed to record the moving water as a soft smoke-like blur.

Acting

I chose a viewpoint which allowed the water to create a diagonal line across the frame and used a long-focus lens to exclude all but the water and immediate foliage. In order to allow the use of a slow shutter speed I set a small aperture and also used a polarising filter to reduce the image brightness even further.

Technique

Sometimes the highlights on backlit water can be too bright to record on film and in this case I used a polarising filter to subdue them as well as helping to create a more translucent quality.

Technique

An alternative method of photographing moving water is to make a series of short exposures onto the same frame of film spaced over a period of a minute or so. If the exposure reading indicates settings of 1/8 sec at f22, for instance, you can obtain the same exposure by giving eight exposures of 1/60 sec at the same aperture or sixteen of 1/125 sec. Naturally, it is vital to use a tripod and to ensure the camera is not moved until the exposure sequence is completed.

Technical Details
35mm Single Lens Reflex - 105mm lens, polariser and 81C warm-up filters 2 sec exposure on Fuji Velvia.

Technical Details
6x4.5cm Single Lens Reflex - 55mm lens, polarising and 81C warm-up filters, Fuji Velvia.

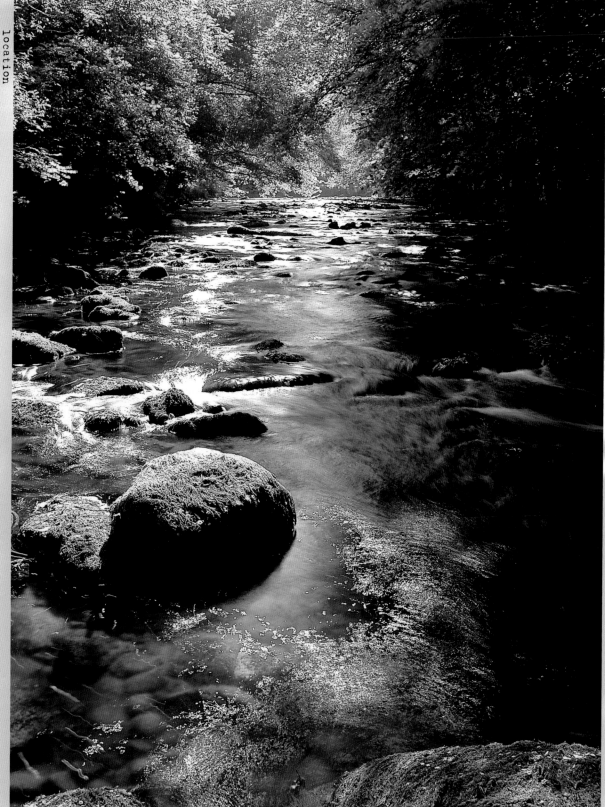

location
The River Cousin - Burgundy, France

Lakes & Mountains

Like the seaside, lakes and mountains can be all things to all people as well as a holiday destination. Whether it is the relaxing atmosphere and beautiful scenery of a summer vacation in the high alps, the energy and excitement of a winter sports holiday, adventure sports or the pleasures of sailing, fishing or boating, the photographic potential is vast, ranging from dramatic landscapes to action photography and nature subjects.

Seeing

It was a crisp, clear day in the French Alps when I passed through this ski resort. There had been a recent fall of snow so the slopes looked quite fresh and white, the sky was a deep, clear blue and the sunlight had a good sharp edge.

Thinking

These are conditions in which more distant views can be successful and I wanted to produce a picture which showed something of both the setting and the activity. The group of skiers waiting for the chair lift seemed to be the obvious choice for a focus of attention and would also provide a much needed element of colour in the image.

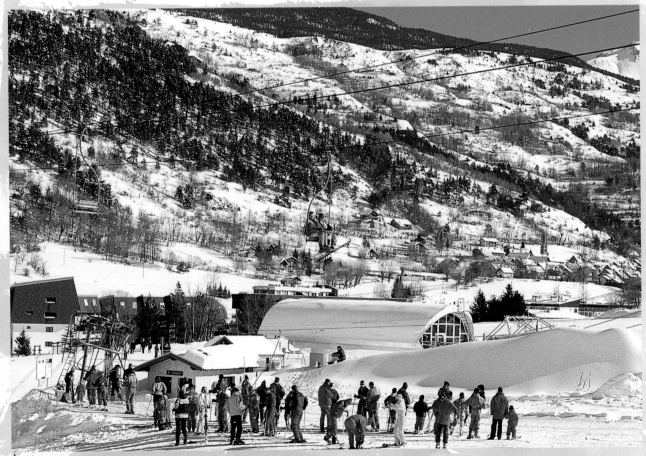

Technical Details
35mm SLR Camera with a 24–85mm zoom lens, 81B warm-up and polarising filters, and Kodak Ektachrome 100 SW.

Acting

I decided to look for a **viewpoint** which would allow me to look down towards the skiers, so I walked a little way up the slope away from them. I **framed the shot**, using a wide-angle lens, in a way which placed the skiers at the **bottom of the frame** with the sky just visible above the distant mountain top.

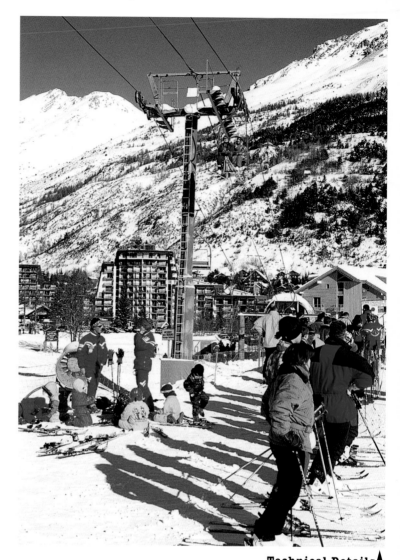

Technical Details
35mm SLR Camera with a 24–85mm zoom lens, 81B warm-up and polarising filters, and Kodak Ektachrome 100 SW.

Technical Details
35mm SLR Camera with a 70–200mm zoom lens, an 81A warm-up filter and Kodak Ektachrome 100 SW.

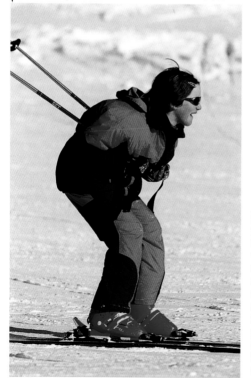

Even without an autofocus camera, photographing action of this type is not so difficult. The secret is to find a good viewpoint which provides a good view of the action, and also places an uncluttered area of the scene in the background, and then determine where your subject should be to create the best composition. You need only then to follow your chosen subject in the viewfinder, panning the camera smoothly to keep pace, and make your exposure, using the fastest practical shutter speed, when he or she arrives in the chosen spot.

I chose a viewpoint for this picture which enabled me to use the line of skiers as foreground interest and framed the shot so that they were on the left-hand side of the frame with the ski lift support more or less in the centre. I waited until a chair arrived at this spot before shooting.

Seeing

I saw this scene on the same lake side as the picture on the opposite page. In this case I was attracted to the powerful contrast between the rich, reddish-coloured wood and the blue water, as well as the pattern which the upright poles of the landing stage had created.

Thinking

I felt that the image would have more impact if I framed the image very tightly and excluded all but the most important details. Limiting the image to just two colours would also place more emphasis on the pattern element of the image.

Acting

I chose a viewpoint which created the best separation between the upright poles and framed it using a long-focus lens, so the sky was excluded, and there was just a small amount of the water below the base of the boats; the pole on the right-hand side of the picture was just included. I used a polarising filter to increase the image's colour saturation.

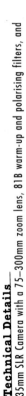

Technical Details
35mm SLR Camera with a 75–300mm zoom lens, 81B warm-up and polarising filters, and Kodak Ektachrome 64.

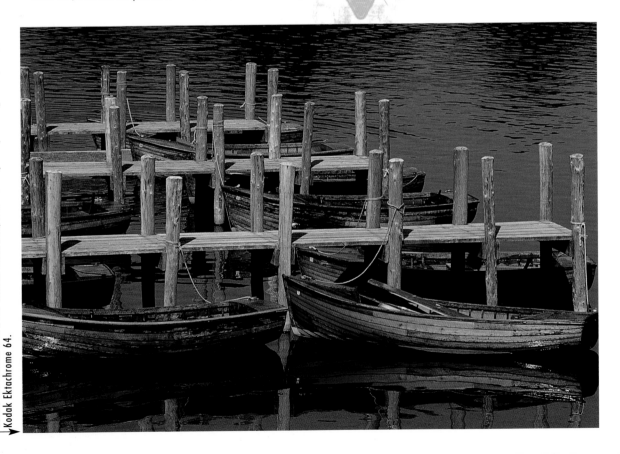

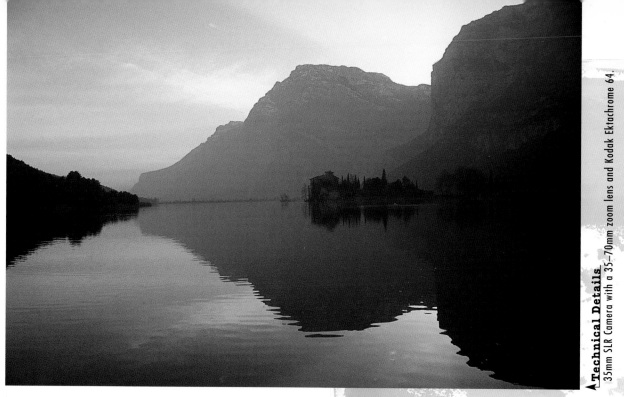

Technical Details
35mm SLR Camera with a 35–70mm zoom lens and Kodak Ektachrome 64.

I took this photograph of Lake Garda in Italy late one winter's afternoon. I was attracted by the fact that the very still water had created an almost mirror-like reflection of the mountains, choosing a viewpoint and framing the shot to emphasise this aspect of the scene. The near-dusk light had created a bluish quality which I thought added to the picture's atmosphere; I did not use a warm-up filter in order to accentuate this.

I used a wide-angle lens for this shot taken in England's Lake District because I wanted to create a strong impression of depth and distance in the picture. This has been emphasised by choosing a viewpoint which placed me close to the boats and framing the image to also include distant details. I used a small aperture to ensure the image was sharp from the nearest to the furthest details.

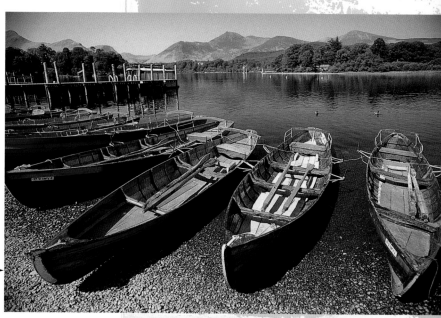

Technical Details
35mm SLR Camera with a 20mm wide-angle lens, 81B warm-up and polarising filters, and Kodak Ektachrome 64.

Lakes & Mountains

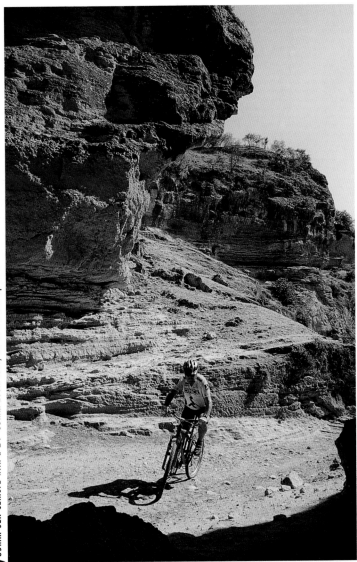

Technical Details
35mm SLR Camera with a 24–85mm zoom lens, an 81B warm-up filter and Kodak Ektachrome 100 SW.

My friend Stuart is a keen mountain biker and frequently goes up into the mountains near Alhama de Granada in Spain's Andalucia region for a day's biking, often in temperatures of over 40°C. On this occasion I accompanied him by car, with a view to shooting some pictures of him in action in the gorges near Alhama. I chose a viewpoint which placed a dramatic area of the cliff behind him and framed the image so that he was at the base of the picture with the rocks towering above.

Seeing

I saw this scene while driving through the Flinders ranges in South Australia's outback. I was **attracted by** the huge old gum tree and the way its leaning trunk and jutting branch **acted as a frame** to the distant mountains.

Thinking

I shot a few **frames of the scene** before realising that it would make a nice **setting for a shot** of the car and this would also add an element of **interest and scale** to the picture.

Acting

I chose a viewpoint which allowed me to **place the tree trunk** to the left of the most prominent peak and the road on the extreme right of the picture. I then asked my friend to drive the car into this spot and, using a **wide-angle lens**, framed the shot so that the jutting branch was just included at the **top of the frame** and the adjacent gum tree on the left was also within the **picture area**.

A very clear day with a strong blue sky and a crystalline atmosphere provided the ideal conditions to shoot this view of the Spanish Pyrenees near the town of Bielsa, where a number of rough tracks lead up high into the mountains. I used a wide-angle lens which allowed me to include some rocks in the close foreground, enhancing the impression of depth and distance. I used a polarising filter to further enhance the image's colour saturation and clarity, and a warm-up filter to counteract the bluish quality which can be created when shooting at high altitudes.

Technical Details
Medium-format SLR Camera with a 55mm wide-angle lens, 81C warm-up and polarising filters, and Fuji Velvia.

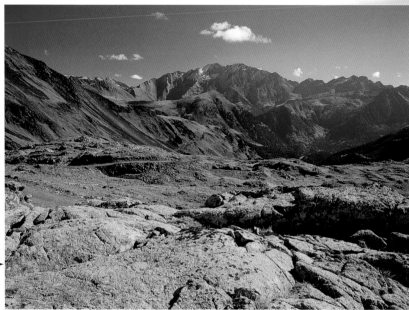

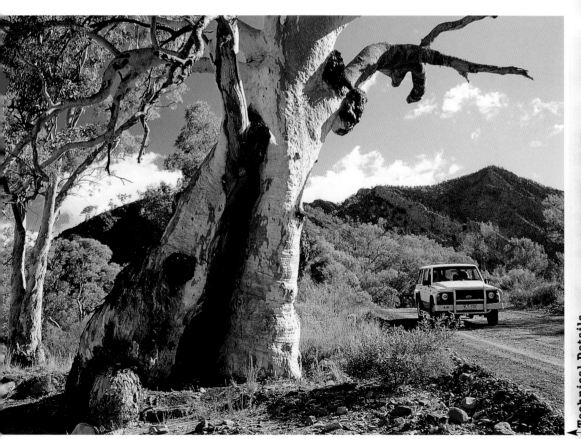

Technical Details
35mm SLR Camera with a 24–85mm zoom lens, 81B warm-up and polarising filters, and Fuji Velvia.

The Coast

The coast offers a wide variety of photogenic possibilities ranging from seascapes to beach scenes, harbours, coastal villages and activities like fishing, wind surfing and sailing. In addition to photographs of broader scenes there are many pictorial possibilities to be found in places like harbours where a closer and more selective approach can produce images with a powerful graphic or abstract quality, such as details of objects like fishing boats, lobster pots and nets, which can add a considerable amount of colour and interest to the photographic coverage of a region.

Seeing

The rich colours of the sunset were the obvious attraction in this scene but I noticed that the reflections in the wet sand, combined with its texture, made the strongest contribution to the image.

It's always worth waiting when shooting sunsets as it's often more effective to wait until the sun has almost disappeared and in some cases stunning colours can be created long after it has set. A good sunset can also vary enormously in colour and quality over a period of time.

Thinking

As I wanted to maximise the effect of the reflections I decided to use a wide-angle lens and to tilt the camera down so the image was dominated by the reflection and only a small area of sky was included.

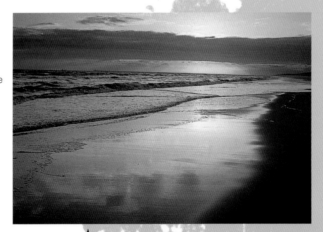

Technical Details
35mm Single Lens Reflex - 24mm lens, neutral-graduated filter, Fuji Velvia.

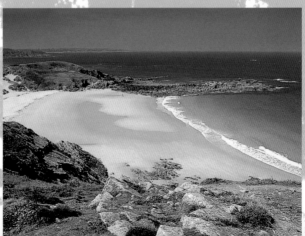

Technical Details
6x4.5cm Single Lens Reflex - 50mm lens, polarising and 81C warm-up filters, Fuji Velvia.

location
A beach near Cap Frehal - Brittany, France

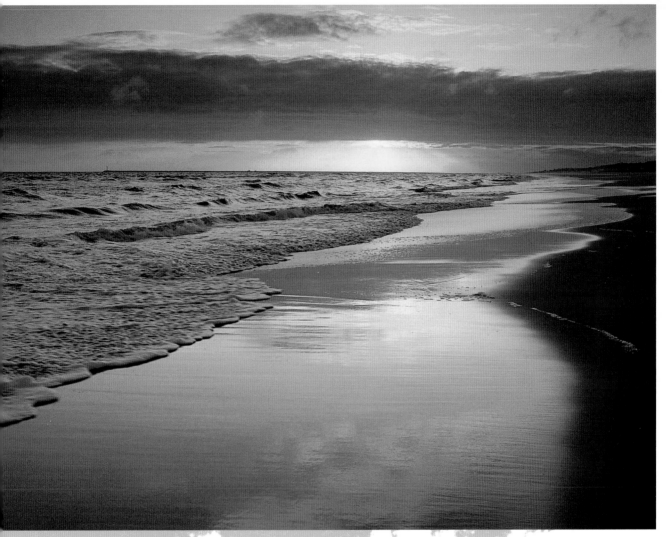

location
The beach at Mazagon - Huelva, Spain

Acting
I chose a viewpoint which allowed me to use the line of the surf as a diagonal and waited until the brightness of the sun was subdued behind cloud before making the exposure. I also used a neutral graduated filter to darken the sky area even more.

Seeing

The sun rising through early morning clouds created a very striking effect in this scene but I felt the image needed some strong foreground interest so I walked along the shore to find this fishing platform.

Thinking

The sky was so much brighter than the foreground and the exposure necessary to record enough detail in the shoreline and fishing platform would have resulted in the cloud effect being over-exposed and losing the drama of the scene.

location
Gironde Estuary - France

Technical Details
6x4.5cm Single Lens Reflex - 55mm lens, neutral-graduated filter, Fuji Velvia.

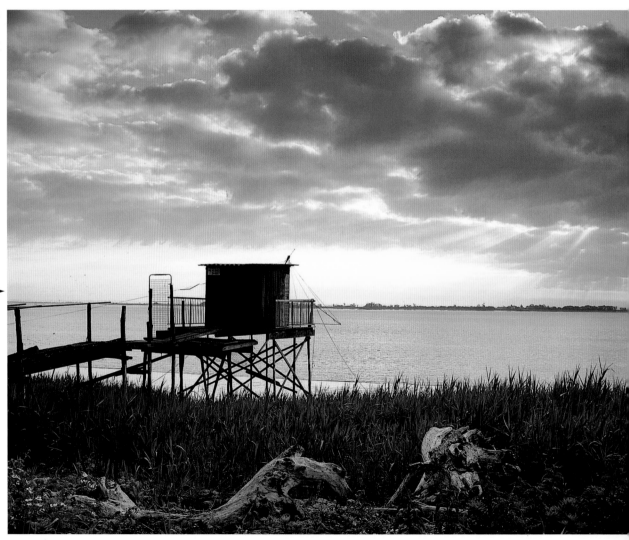

Rule of Thumb

When shooting subjects close to the camera it's best to use a small aperture as depth of field decreases quite considerably when the camera is focused at close distances. An image like this pile of lobster pots needs to be really sharp overall to be effective.

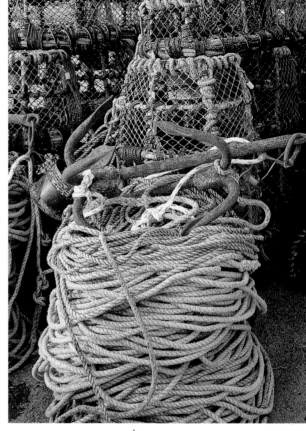

location
Barfleur - Normandy, France

Acting

I chose a

viewpoint

which placed the most effective area of the sky behind the fishing platform and used a wide-angle lens to include some of the shoreline detail as well as the cloud effect. I fitted a neutral

graduated filter to enable

me to give enough exposure to record foreground detail

without over-exposing the

sky.

Technical Details
6x4.5cm Single Lens Reflex - 55mm lens, 81A filter, 1/4 sec @ f22, Fuji Velvia.

When composing a shot it helps to look first at the edges of the frame rather than the centre, which is the natural reaction, as it helps you to avoid including any distracting details.

Technical Details
35mm Single Lens Reflex - 35mm lens, polarising and 81C warm-up filters, Fuji Velvia.

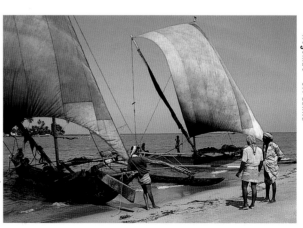

location
Negombo - Sri Lanka

The Seaside

Probably the most popular of all holiday destinations, the seaside offers the greatest variety of opportunities for interesting and colourful photography, ranging from beach activities and seascapes to harbours and fishing boats, together with all the photogenic trappings of the seaside, such as rock pools, beach huts, deck chairs and lighthouses. It is also one of the easiest situations in which to produce muddled and unsatisfying pictures unless you are very selective and compose your pictures with care.

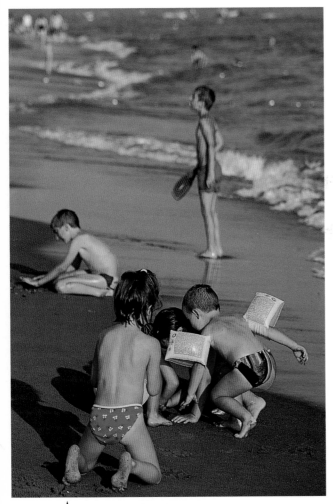

▲Technical Details
35mm SLR Camera with a 70–210mm zoom lens and Kodak Ektachrome 100 SW.

Seeing

I'd been watching this group of children playing on a beach in Spain's Costa del Sol for a while thinking that there was the possibility of a picture. But the beach was very busy and there were too many people around the children and also behind them in the sea.

Thinking

I felt sure that if I waited long enough the area would clear a little and if I found the right viewpoint I might be able to separate the group I was interested in from their surroundings.

Acting

I suddenly saw my opportunity from a spot where the background was much less cluttered and the children were placed in quite a pleasing arrangement. I used a long-focus lens to crop the image quite tightly and to exclude as many unwanted details as possible.

Rule of Thumb

You need to take extra care of your equipment when shooting on a beach as both salt water spray and sand can cause considerable damage to cameras and lenses. It is wise to keep each item in a sealed plastic bag inside your camera case until needed.

Technical Details
▼ 35mm SLR Camera with a 75–300mm zoom lens, an 81A warm-up filter and Fuji Velvia.

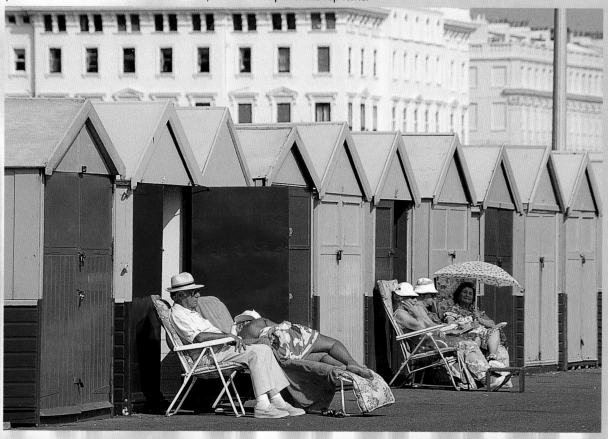

This photograph was taken on the promenade at Hove in Sussex, UK. I was attracted by the juxtaposition of the rather garish beach huts and background of quite elegant facades. I chose a viewpoint which allowed me to include the group of holiday makers and one which was distant enough to make the background houses rise above the roofs of the huts. I needed to use a long-focus lens to enlarge the most interesting area of the scene.

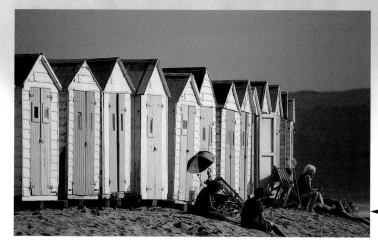

These beach huts were at Woolacombe in North Devon, UK, and I chose a quite distant viewpoint at a fairly acute angle to the row of huts and used a long-focus lens in order to create the impression of compressed perspective.

◄ **Technical Details**
35mm SLR Camera with a 75–300mm zoom lens, an 81A warm-up filter and Fuji Velvia.

Seeing

These catamaran fishing boats were pulled up onto the beach at Negombo in Sri Lanka. I was initially attracted by the **contrast** between their **rust-brown** sails and the deep blue sky and started to look for a suitable **viewpoint**.

Thinking

As I **studied** the scene more carefully I realised that the distant palm trees and the **red-roofed hut** could be used to add interest to the image and would also show more of the **location** and its atmosphere.

Acting

From this spot, I found I could create enough **separation** between the two sails and at the same time place the **palm trees** and red roof just to one side of them. I **framed** the shot to include all of the boats but tightly enough on the right-hand side to **exclude** a parked truck which rather spoilt the **mood** of the picture.

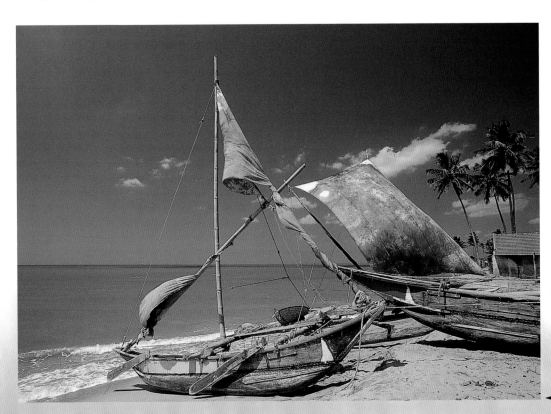

Technical Details 35mm SLR Camera with a 28–70mm zoom lens, 81B warm-up and polarising filters, and Fuji Velvia.

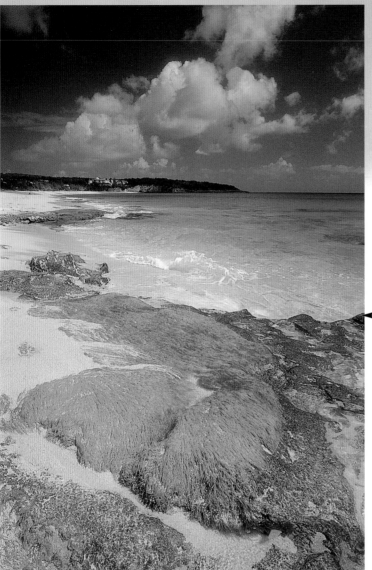

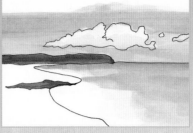

Even the most stunning beach will not produce a good picture unless you take measures to create a pleasing composition. Often the most effective way is to find an interesting foreground, like these colourful rocks on a Caribbean beach. This will introduce a much needed element of contrast to the sand and sky and help to give the image a sense of depth and distance. This shows how using the upright format has allowed a much larger area of foreground to be included adding both depth and impact to the image.

Technical Details
35mm SLR Camera with a 20–35mm zoom lens, 81B warm-up and polarising filters, and Fuji Velvia.

Looking more closely at a scene is often an effective way of producing pictures with a difference and adding variety to photographs taken at the seaside. These limpets were on a rock in North Devon, UK, and I used a macro lens to allow me to focus closely enough to fill the frame with a small area to reveal the rich texture and detail of the shell.

Technical Details
35mm SLR Camera with a 90mm macro lens, an 81A warm-up filter and Fuji Velvia.

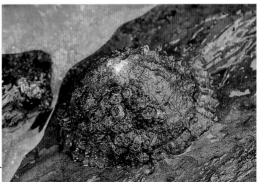

The Seaside

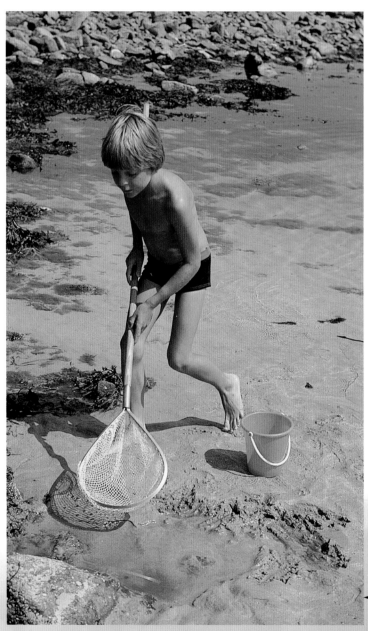

Rule of Thumb

When photographing people in this way, having an interesting but unobtrusive background is usually a major factor in the success of the picture. It's best to move around your subject looking for a viewpoint where this can be combined with a pleasing angle on your subject.

Many people will set up holiday pictures of their friends and family, making them stop what they are doing and look at the camera, but it is often far more pleasing to take pictures with as little disturbance of the subject as possible, and having someone looking self-consciously into the camera will usually detract from the mood of the occasion. With this picture I simply tracked my young subject for a while as he was engrossed in his fishing until he moved into a spot where there was an effective background and he adopted a nice pose.

◀ Technical Details

35mm SLR Camera with a 35–70mm zoom lens, an 81A warm-up filter and Kodak Kodachrome 64.

Seeing

I saw this colourful assemblage of seaside equipment on a beach in the Italian Riviera and was immediately struck by the pleasing mix of bright, bold colours.

Thinking

I realised that, unless I was very careful, the outcome could easily be a muddle with each colour vying for attention, and the resulting image suffering from an unbalanced composition.

Acting

I decided that the best approach was to be very selective and not to try and get too much into the subject. I found this viewpoint where, even by cropping the image quite tightly with a long-focus lens, I was able to include enough of each of the key details of the scene to create a balanced composition without losing the essence of the place.

Technical Details

▼ Medium-format SLR Camera with a 150mm lens, an 81A warm-up filter and Kodak Ektachrome 64.

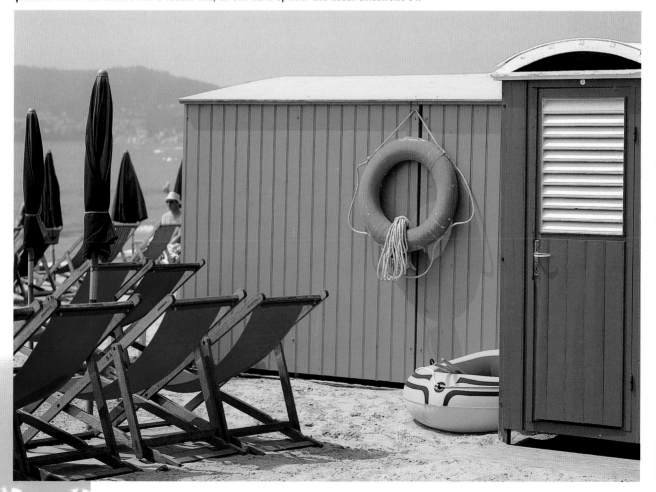

Technical Details →
6x4.5cm Single Lens Reflex - 105-
210mm lens, polarising and 81C
warm-up filters, Fuji Velvia.

Photographing the world's most famous landmarks can be a problem if only because they have been very well photographed many times before and are familiar to all. But such images are in regular demand by editors and publishers and a strong image of a well-known place will always find a market.

Seeing

The row of windmills lining the ridge of a hill above the village of Consuegra are hard to miss but finding a viewpoint which groups them into a pleasing arrangement is a little more difficult.

Thinking

I felt that my best chance of grouping several together was to find a viewpoint which allowed me to shoot along the ridge. This was made more difficult as the angle of the strong directional sunlight created unattractive lighting effects from some of the possible viewpoints and there was a tarmac road quite near them which I wanted to exclude.

Acting

I found this viewpoint by climbing onto a rocky knoll some distance away from the windmills but found that my 210mm lens enabled me to frame them quite tightly and also allowed me to crop out the tarmac in the immediate foreground.

Technique

If they are Illuminated, buildings will often look more interesting when shot at night than they do in daylight and this can also be a very useful way of masking problems like crowds of people, parked cars and street signs, for instance.

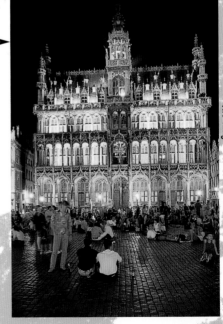

Technical Details →
35mm Single Lens Reflex -
28mm perspective control lens,
1/2 sec at f5.6, Fuji Provia
rated at ISO 200.

location
The King's House, Market Place - Brussels, Belgium

Technical Details
6x4.5cm Single Lens Reflex -
105-210mm zoom lens,
81B warm-up filter, Fuji Velvia.

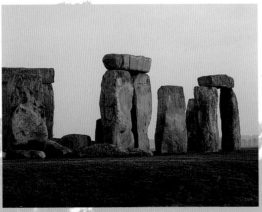

When photographing well-known places it often helps to give your pictures more impact and to avoid the pictures postcard cliches if you shoot when the lighting or weather conditions are unusual - as in this shot of Stonehenge taken just before a summer storm.

location
Stonehenge - Wiltshire, UK

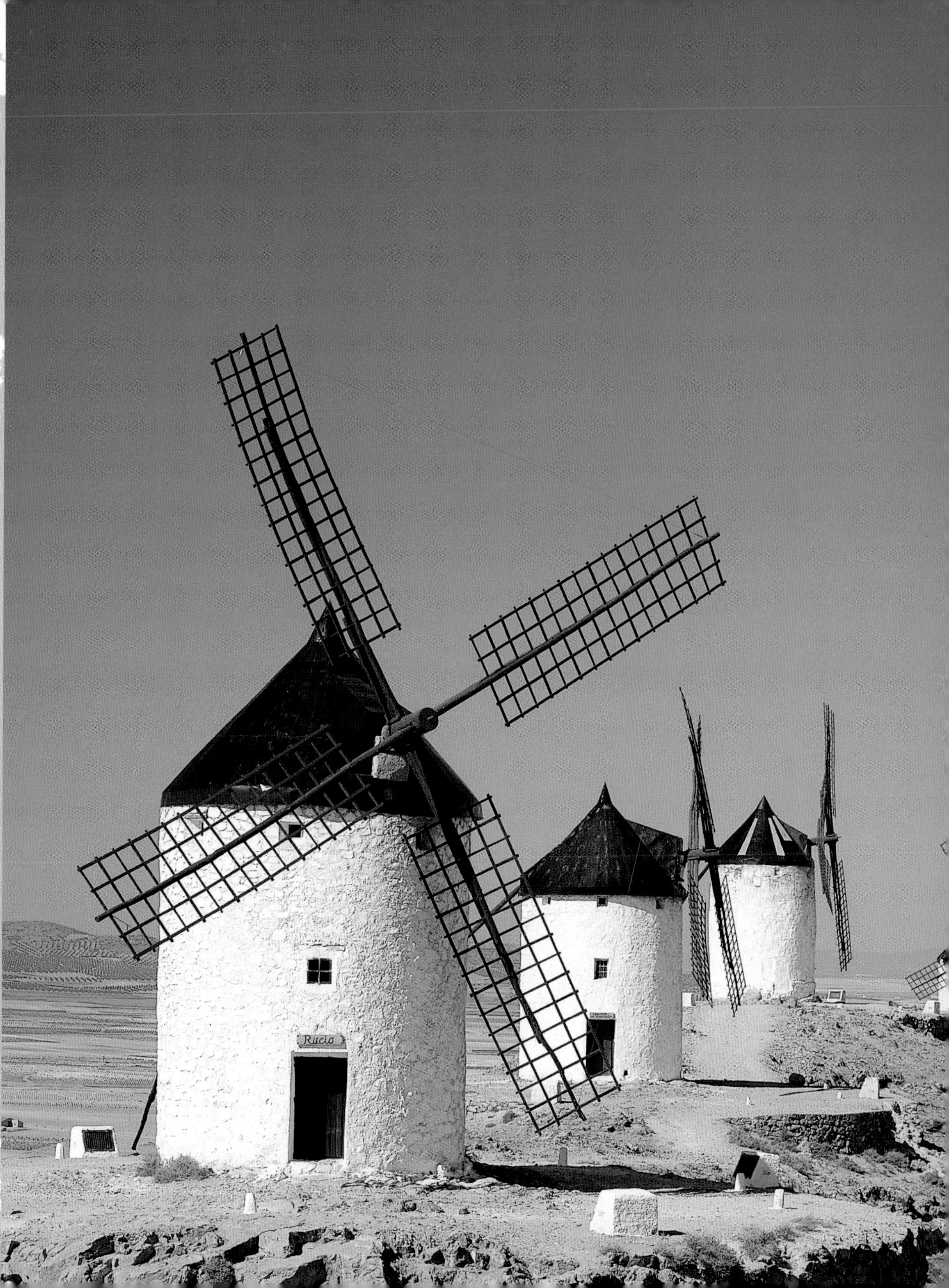

location
Consuegra - La Mancha, Spain

Familiar Landmarks

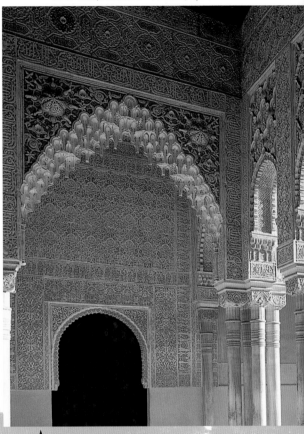

Rule of Thumb

A perspective control lens not only enables you to include the top of a tall building without the need to tilt the camera upwards, causing converging verticals, but it can also sometimes be effective to use it to exclude a cluttered or uninteresting foreground.

Technical Details
35mm Single Lens Reflex - 28mm perspective control lens, Fuji Velvia.

location
Taj Mahal - Agra India

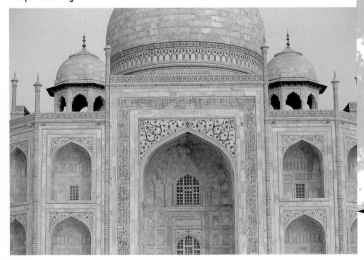

Technical Details
35mm Single Lens Reflex - 75-300mm zoom lens, 81B warm-up filter, Fuji Velvia.

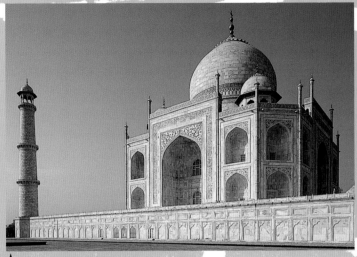

Technical Details
35mm Single Lens Reflex - 28mm perspective control lens, 81A warm-up filter, Fuji Velvia.

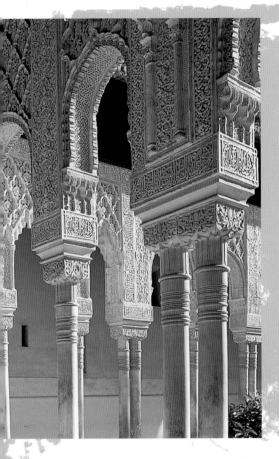

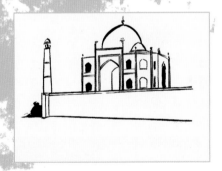

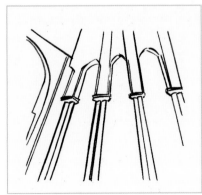

Finding a less familiar viewpoint is often helpful in producing a strong image of a well-known site. The Lions Court in the Alhambra is almost always photographed from the exterior courtyard looking in but this shot taken from inside looking out presents a more unusual image. The diagram shows the effect which would have been created if the camera had been tilted upwards instead of using a perspective control lens.

Centuries old buildings, whether they are
churches, castles, palaces or simple cottages,
usually have a number of things in common - ancient stonework, weathered timbers
and ornate decorations. These provide the the sort of visual components with which
the photographic process can be used to create images with a
rich, textural quality and powerful sense of form and depth.

The colour, and texture, of old stone and
timber is greatly enhanced by the warm,
mellow sunlight created at the end of the
day and if the building's outlook, and the
chosen viewpoint permits, this is usually
the best time to shoot. If using the bluer
quality of light in the middle of the day is
unavoidable it can be of huge benefit to
use a strong warm-up filter, like an 81C or
81EF, for example.

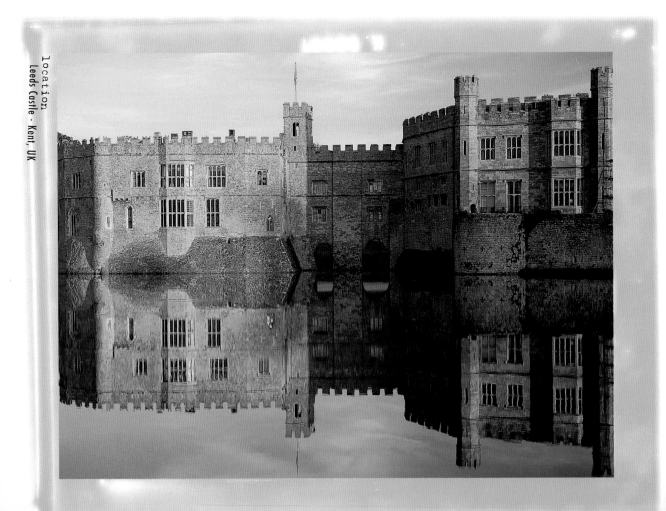

location
Leeds Castle - Kent, UK

Acting

I found that walking to the far side of the square I was just able to include all of the building using my 28mm perspective control lens with it shifted upwards, almost to its maximum extent. I also found that if I went slightly further back into the arcade which runs along this side of the square I could also include enough of the arch to act as a frame to the image.

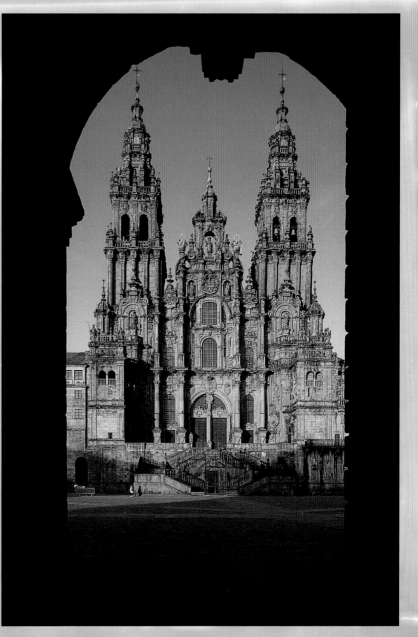

Seeing

The warm quality light of evening light and its glancing angle across the facade of the building created a very striking quality which I felt needed only a straightforward approach to record it successfully.

Thinking

I wanted to show the complete facade of the cathedral and also to photograph it front on. I felt it was necessary to avoid the converging verticals which would have been caused by tilting the camera upwards to include the top of the structure.

Technical Details →
35mm Single Lens Reflex - 28mm perspective control lens, Fuji Velvia.

← Technical Details
6x4.5cm Single Lens Reflex - 55-110 zoom lens, 81A warm-up filter, Fuji Velvia.

Historic Buildings

Technical Details
35mm Single Lens Reflex - 35-70mm zoom lens, neutral-graduated and 81C warm-up filters, Fuji Velvia.

Technical Details
6x4.5cm Single Lens Reflex - 50mm lens, polarising and 81EF warm-up filters, Fuji Velvia.

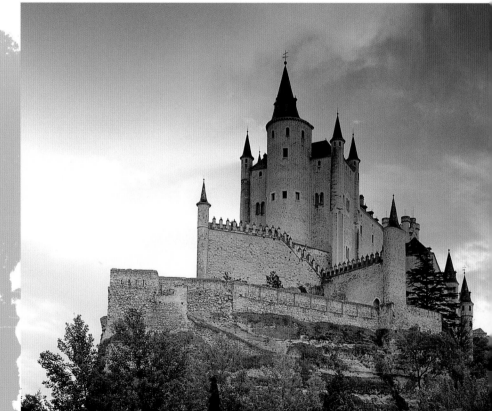

location
The Alcazar, Segovia - Castile Leon, Spain

Titling the camera up to include the top of a building and deliberately causing converging verticals can often be effective but it's best not to include the ground or horizon as this can make the building appear to be toppling backwards.

When looking for a more distant viewpoint of a building it can help to stand in front of the aspect you want to photograph and look for suitable places which are accessible - a pair of binoculars are often helpul.

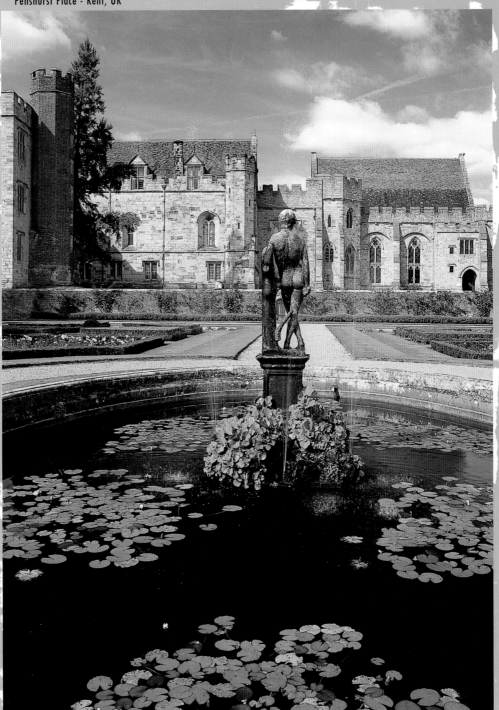

Photographing the Sights

Famous sights and well-known landmarks must account for a large proportion of the photographs people take when travelling on vacation. Quite a few of these are of the variety where a companion is pictured with a famous sight behind them, but apart from providing evidence on the "Been there, done that" level there has always seemed little point in it to me. Far better, I would think, to take away a picture as a souvenir which was personalised more by being an original or appealing image of a place. These also have the benefit of being of much greater interest to others who look at them.

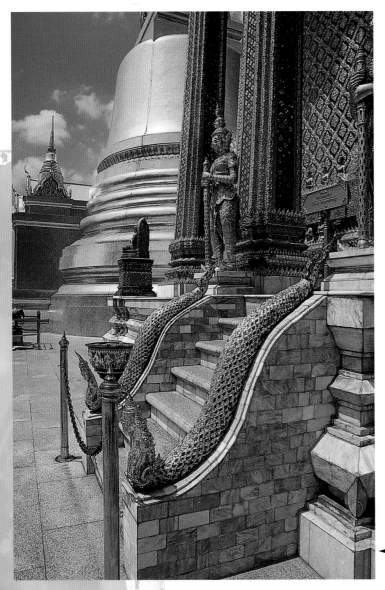

Seeing

The Grand Palace in Bangkok is top of the hit list for tourists and I made the mistake of not going there first thing in the morning, so by the time I arrived it was teeming with people. The sky was also rather hazy and consequently the scene lacked the sharpness and clarity I would have liked.

Thinking

Because of this I decided to try looking for shots of more selective areas and ones which showed some of the detail and texture of the palace buildings.

Acting

I used a wide-angle lens and viewpoint close to this foreground of the steps, limiting the area into which passing visitors could stray into my frame. This exaggerated the perspective and enhanced the three-dimensional quality of the image.

Technical Details
35mm SLR Camera with a 24–85mm zoom lens, an 81A warm-up filter and Fuji Velvia.

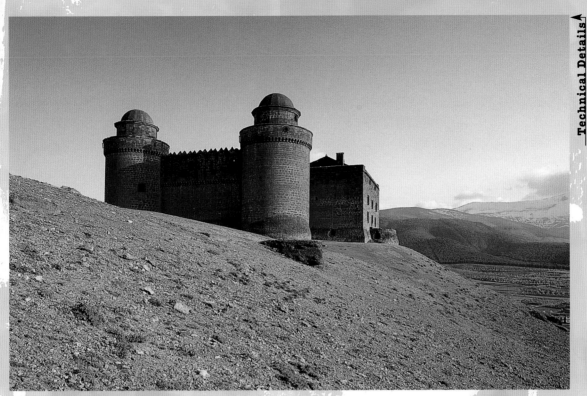

Technical Details
35mm SLR Camera with a 28mm shift lens, 81A warm-up and polarising filters, and Fuji Velvia.

This is the castle of Lacalahorra in Spain's Andalucia. It's perched on a hilltop above a village of white houses and this is how it's usually pictured in guide books and postcards. I arrived there late one afternoon and climbed up to the castle to find that the warm sunlight was turning the stone of the castle walls a rich colour which contrasted quite strongly with the deep blue sky. I found that from this viewpoint I could avoid including any other details and this gave the place the remote and isolated atmosphere I imagine the occupants once had.

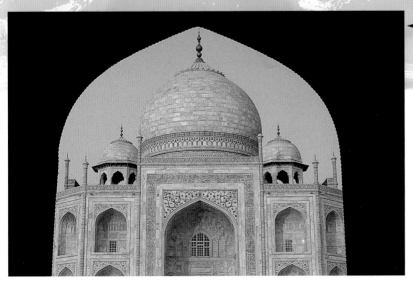

Technical Details
35mm SLR Camera with a 35–70mm zoom lens, an 81A warm-up filter and Fuji Velvia.

The simple expedient of photographing the side of the Taj Mahal, in India, and using a doorway as a frame to the image makes this shot a little less familiar than most.

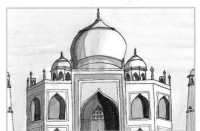

Photographing the Sights

Seeing

A friend recommended a hotel in Sydney, Australia, when I told him I'd planned to visit. He said it had a good view of Sydney Harbour Bridge. He was not wrong. The first of my three days' stay, however, was very grey, cloudy and rainy with no opportunity to make use of my bedroom window viewpoint. The second day had a brief period of sunlight in the afternoon and I made use of that, but the shot was nothing very special.

Thinking

There are so many good photographs of this bridge that I almost felt inclined to not shoot it at all in spite of the heaven-sent gift of a good viewpoint. But I reasoned that it only needed a more interesting light to give me an image I could be happy with.

Acting

The sun was rising very early at this time of year but, in spite of harrowing jet lag, I set my alarm for 4.30 AM. Staggering to the window I was delighted to discover that the previous evening's cloud had cleared and there was colour on the eastern horizon. I set up and waited using a wide-angle lens with my panoramic camera. This format was ideal as both the sky and the water became black very quickly further from the horizon and would have produced a large, featureless area on a standard landscape.

Technical Details
▼35mm Viewfinder Camera with a 45mm wide-angle lens and Fuji Velvia.

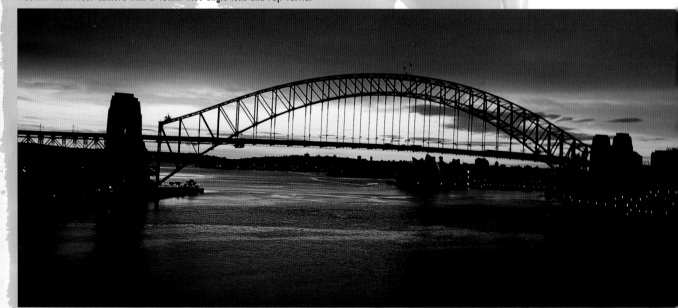

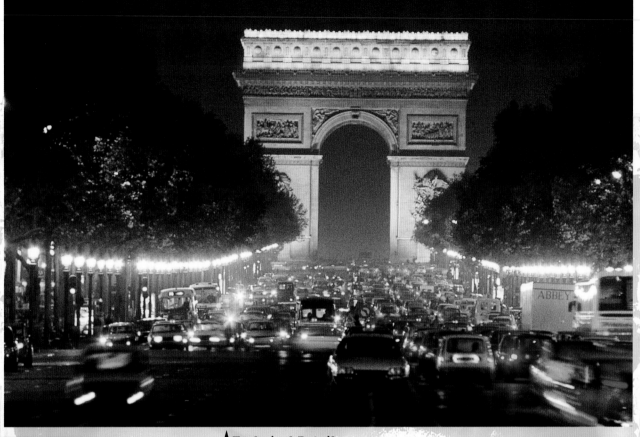

↑**Technical Details**
35mm SLR Camera with a 75–300mm zoom lens, an 81A warm-up filter and Kodak Ektachrome

The problems of obstructions such as crowds of people and parked cars can often be overcome by shooting at night when a building is well illuminated. This picture of the Arc de Triomphe in Paris was taken from a road island in the middle of the Champs Elysées, using a long-focus lens to enlarge the most effective part of the scene. I used a tripod to support the camera for the necessary exposure of several seconds.

Rule of Thumb

There's often a desire when shooting famous sights to try and include all of the structure and this is where the choice of viewpoint and even the lighting can be a very restricting factor. Instead, if you consider the building or monument to simply be something of which you can use as little or as much as necessary to make a satisfying image, you will find that this can give your pictures a more interesting quality than would a straightforward architectural record.

Photographing the Sights

Seeing

I had visited the Victoria falls in Zimbabwe during the afternoon of the previous day and had been mightily impressed – it's a truly awe-inspiring sight – but recognised that this was not going to translate into an even moderately interesting photograph at that particular time, as it was cloudy and the viewpoints were very limited at this point of access.

Thinking

I was moving on the next day with the group I was accompanying but thought I would have time, and that it might be worthwhile, to go very early again to the falls before the sun rose, and shoot if the sky looked clear.

Acting

At 4.00 AM there was not a cloud in the sky and I set off, arriving at this viewpoint ten minutes or so before the sun lifted above the artificial horizon of the falls. I shot a few pictures at this time and they were quite pleasing but decided to wait to see where the sun would rise. As you can see, it rose blindingly bright directly ahead of me and I fitted a wide-angle lens and a neutral-graduated filter to tone it down a little and made a few exposures. In less than a minute or so the sun was far too bright causing flare and obliterating the rest of the scene. At this point I was not really sure if I had anything worthwhile, but on processing the film I felt that there was just enough sense of the mass of cascading water and the colour and atmosphere of sunrise to make it work.

Technical Details
▼35mm SLR Camera with a 20–35mm zoom lens, a neutral-graduated filter and Fuji Velvia.

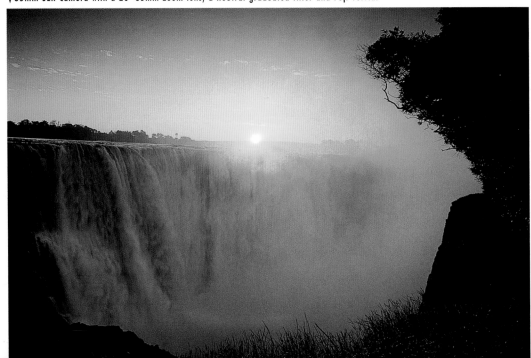

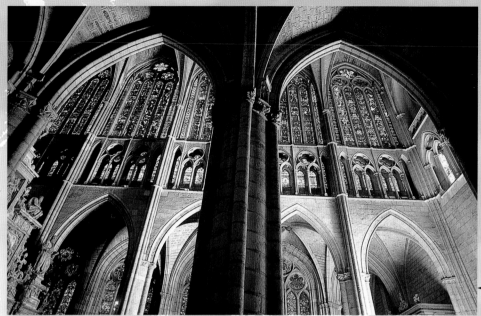

I photographed this section of the interior of the Cathedral of Leon in Spain using just natural light, choosing a viewpoint and framing the image to exclude any very bright or very dark areas.

▶ **Technical Details**
35mm SLR Camera with a 20–35mm zoom lens and Fuji Velvia.

Technical Tip

When shooting into the light there is a strong possibility that the camera's exposure meter will read the scene as being much brighter than it really is, especially when the sun is included in the image. This will cause under-exposure if not corrected. The best solution is to take a close-up reading from a mid-grey tone in the foreground of the scene or to increase the exposure indicated by a normal average reading by between one and three stops depending on the brightness of the back-lighting.

Shooting very early in the morning is often well worth the effort when photographing well-known places. Firstly, it overcomes the problem of crowds of sightseers – few are around before breakfast – and secondly the warm colour quality of low-angled sunlight invariably enhances the colour, texture and ambience of old stone and weathered wood. This shot of London's Big Ben was taken from a viewpoint on Westminster Bridge and I framed the picture to exclude the passing traffic.

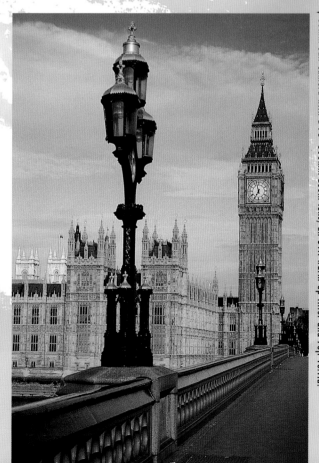

▼ **Technical Details**
35mm SLR Camera with a 75–300mm zoom lens, an 81A warm-up filter and Fuji Velvia.

Countryside & Villages

One of my greatest pleasures is driving through unspoilt countryside with a good map and the time to explore. The most enjoyable experiences and most memorable times are frequently those which result from a chance discovery of a charming village or quiet scenic route which are not in the guide books, and these are often the occasions when you take the photographs you are most pleased with.

I saw this scene in the small New England village of Wilmington, USA. It seemed to contain all the ingredients which characterise these villages: white clapper-board houses, wooden decks, country crafts and an American flag. I framed the shot tightly to emphasise these elements and included enough of the green tree and blue sky to create a contrast.

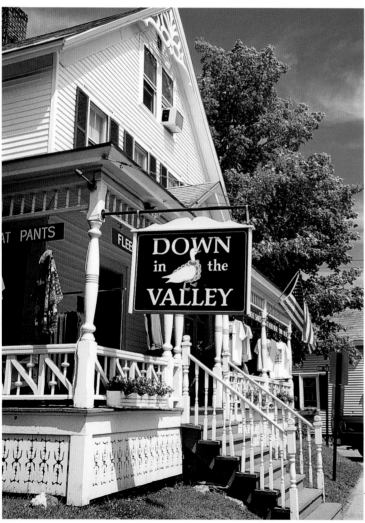

Seeing

In fact, this village green is quite close to my home and I was driving past early one summer's morning when I saw this game in progress. The way the distant church and the fresh, green foliage were lit by the sunlight, still quite low in the sky, were the factors which appealed to me about the scene.

Thinking

I set about looking for a viewpoint which would incorporate these elements most effectively. From this spot I could include the overhanging branch from the nearest tree and it also gave me a good three-quarter view of the wicket and separated the players quite well.

Acting

I framed the shot so that the overhanging branch filled the top right quarter of the frame and there was a comfortable amount of space on the other side of the church. I then waited until there was a moment of action before making my exposure.

Technical Details
35mm Viewfinder Camera with a 45mm lens, an 81B warm-up filter and Fuji Provia.

I found this corner in the very pretty village of Gerberoy in the Picardy region of France. It was an overcast day but the soft lighting was ideal for this close-up shot, which appealed to me because of the rich colours and textures of the stone and foliage.

Technical Details
Medium-format SLR Camera with a 55–105mm zoom lens, an 81A warm-up filter and Fuji Velvia.

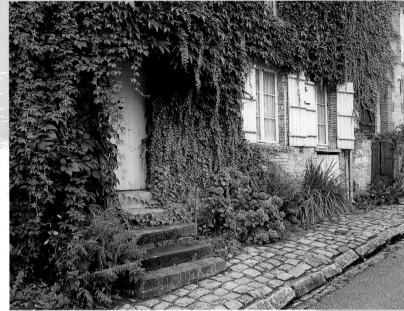

Technical Details
Medium-format SLR Camera with a 210mm lens, 81C warm-up and polarising filters, and Fuji Velvia.

Countryside & Villages

Seeing

I always think that the late autumn is the best time to visit and photograph the countryside and this is especially true of wine country when the vines turn this wonderful colour of burnished gold. It's seldom bettered than in the Champagne region of France where this picture was taken.

Thinking

I wanted to show as large an expanse of the vines as possible and decided to look for a high viewpoint which would enable me to look down the vine rows to the distant plain. Looking across the vine rows usually results in a rather featureless expanse of colour.

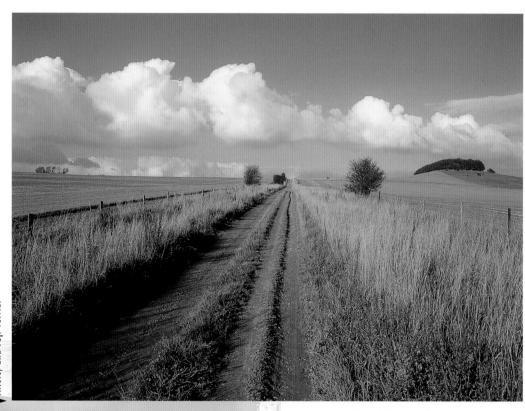

Technical Details
Medium-format SLR Camera with a 50mm wide-angle lens, 81B warm-up and polarising filters, and Fuji Velvia.

Walking is one of the most popular and enjoyable ways of experiencing the countryside and this picture shows a section of the Ridgeway, one of the best-loved long-distance tracks in England. It was a crisp, early-winter's morning and the sunlight was at a low angle, sharp and clear. I liked the 'V' shape created by the grasses lining the track and the way the latter disappeared into the distance — I thought it looked inviting. I chose a viewpoint just to one side of the track's centre and used a wide-angle lens to heighten the perspective effect and give a strong feeling of depth and distance.

Technical Details
35mm SLR Camera with a 75–300mm zoom lens, 81B warm-up, neutral-graduated and polarising filters, and Fuji Velvia.

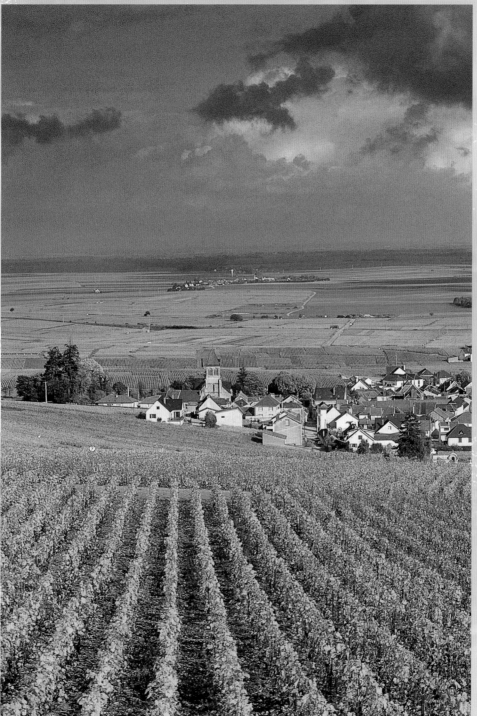

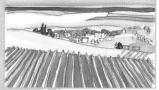

Acting

From this spot I found that I could **achieve** this and also include the village which I thought would provide an **effective focus** of interest for the **composition**. I also chose to include a generous area of the **grey sky** to balance the composition and enhance the effect of the golden vines, so I used the **upright format**, placing the village just below the centre of the frame. Using the landscape shape for this scene would have meant including much less of the sky and foreground and would have diminished the effect of the picture.

Rule of Thumb

Using a wide-angle lens and a viewpoint which includes close foreground details will help to produce pictures which have a three-dimensional quality and a feeling of depth, but you must use a small aperture if you want both foreground and horizon detail to be sharp.

Seeing

I spotted this old cottage in the village of Gerberoy in France late one afternoon and was attracted by the way the light glanced along the cobbled street creating a rich texture.

Thinking

Although the houses beside the cobbles were very pretty they were in shadow and I felt that another element was needed to create a strong image. I therefore looked for a viewpoint that would allow me to include some foreground interest.

Acting

Opposite the houses was a small covered-market hall and I found that by setting my camera up just inside it, and using a wide-angle lens, I was able to include enough of one of the archways to act as a frame around the cottages, which gave the image that extra edge it needed.

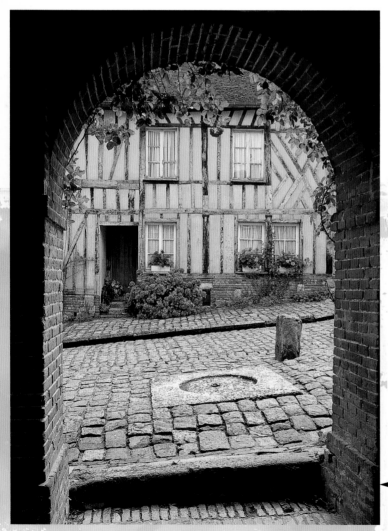

Rule of Thumb

The warm, mellow sunlight early or late in the day is ideal for photographing buildings, especially those built of ancient stone and weathered wood, as it enriches the colour and enhances the texture.

Technical Details

Medium-format SLR Camera with a 50mm wide-angle lens and an 81A warm-up filter.

The village of Labastide d'Armagnac is one of the most photogenic mediaeval villages in France with a central square surrounded by ancient houses, stone arcades and a fine old church. I took this picture early on a Sunday morning when few people were around. I chose this viewpoint as it gave me a pleasing perspective on the fronts of the houses and also, by using a wide-angle lens, allowed me to include some of the arcade as foreground, helping to create a feeling of depth in the picture as well as adding interest to the composition.

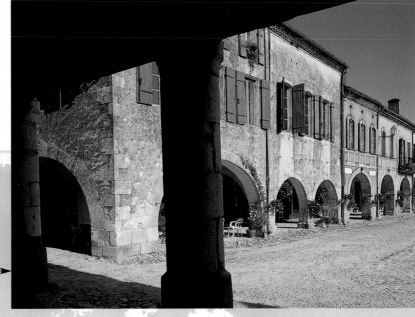

Technical Details

Medium-format SLR Camera with a 50mm wide-angle lens, 81B warm-up and polarising filters, and Fuji Velvia.

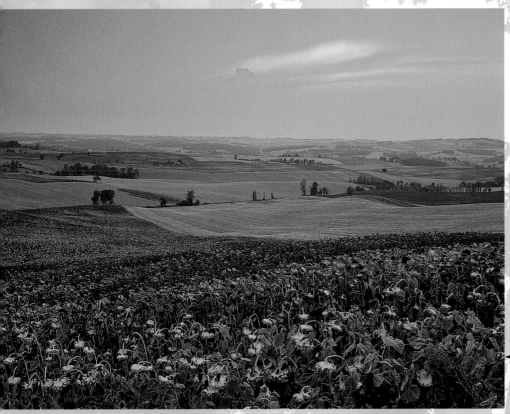

This autumnal landscape was photographed in the Gascony region of France, and the field in the foreground is of sunflowers which have died off and are waiting to be harvested. It had been a dull, overcast day and it was not until a short while before sunset that the sun began to make a weak appearance. It broke through the cloud just enough to create this subtle colour in the sky which together with the autumnal colours created an almost old-fashioned, sepia effect.

Technical Details

Medium-format SLR Camera with a 55–110mm zoom lens, 81A warm-up and neutral-graduated filters, and Fuji Velvia.

Towns & Cities

City breaks have become a very popular form of vacation and have the advantage that they can be enjoyed at any time of the year. They are also much less weather dependent than many other types of holiday and this is reflected in the photographic possibilities, as the colourful and lively nature of city life can provide plenty of opportunities when the weather is dull, as well as creating the opportunity for taking interesting photographs after dark.

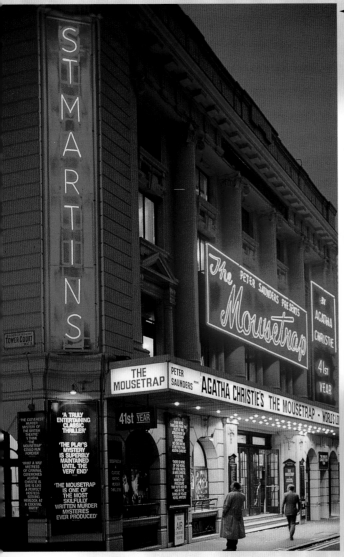

Technical Details

35mm SLR Camera with a 75–300mm zoom lens and Fuji Provia.

This photograph was taken in London's theatre land not long after the sun had gone down. I used a long-focus lens to frame the image tightly, restricting the image to the most strongly lit part of the scene and excluding any especially dark areas which lacked detail.

I took this photograph in the lively old streets of Brussels on a summer evening. The street was very well lit and some weak daylight remained, but, although the scene was predominately lit by artificial light, I opted to use daylight-type transparency film because I thought the resulting orange colour-cast would contribute to the image's atmosphere.

Technical Details

35mm SLR Camera with a 24–85mm zoom lens and Fuji Provia.

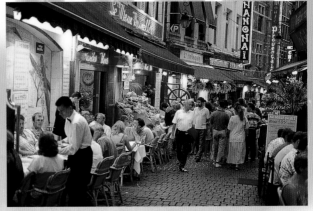

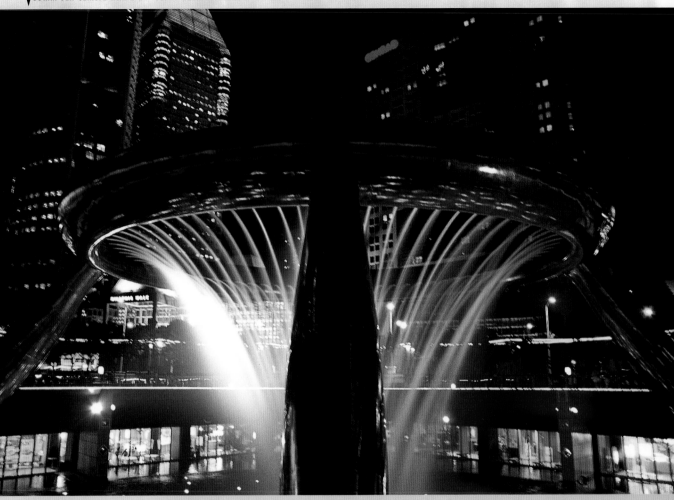

Seeing

This is Singapore's Fountain of Wealth, reputed to be the largest of its kind in the world. At certain hours, the computer-controlled fountain is turned into a sort of aquatic fireworks display in which the ever changing patterns created by the jets of water are lit by multi-coloured lasers.

Thinking

During my visit the first display of the evening was long after sunset and the sky was completely dark. The only way to overcome this was to look for a viewpoint from which I could place the most strongly illuminated area of the background immediately behind the fountain.

Acting

I then framed the image in a way that excluded all the darker areas of the scene, waiting before shooting until the laser display lit the water most evenly. My difficulty was compounded by the fact that I did not have my tripod with me and the exposure needed was in the order of two seconds. I managed to find a lamppost close to my chosen viewpoint and was able to brace the camera firmly enough against it to avoid camera shake.

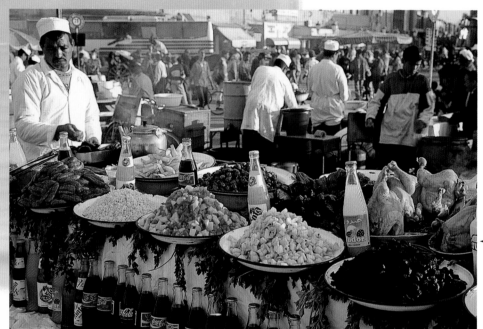

Street life is a feature of the urban environment which can be particularly rewarding for photographers and will help to create a sense of place in a record of a city. This picture was taken in the main square of Marrakech, Morocco, where in the evenings, dozens of small food stalls are set up with a mouth-watering variety of delicacies to sample. I used a long-focus lens to isolate a small section of the scene and used a wide aperture so the background details were slightly soft and not too intrusive.

Technical Details
35mm SLR Camera with a 20–35mm zoom lens, an 81A warm-up filter and Fuji Velvia.

Technical Details
35mm SLR Camera with a 28mm shift lens, an 81A warm-up filter and Fuji Provia.

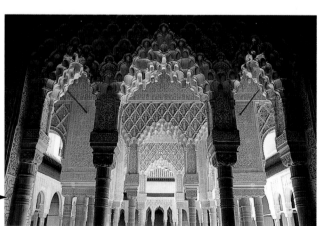

This photograph is of the Lion's Court in the Alhambra Palace in Granada, Spain. I used a wide-angle lens and tilted the camera upwards to create a deliberate distortion. I took care to avoid showing the base of the building as this tends to make tilted camera pictures look awkward.

Technical Details
35mm SLR Camera with a 24–85mm zoom lens, an 81A warm-up filter and Kodak Ektachrome 100 SW.

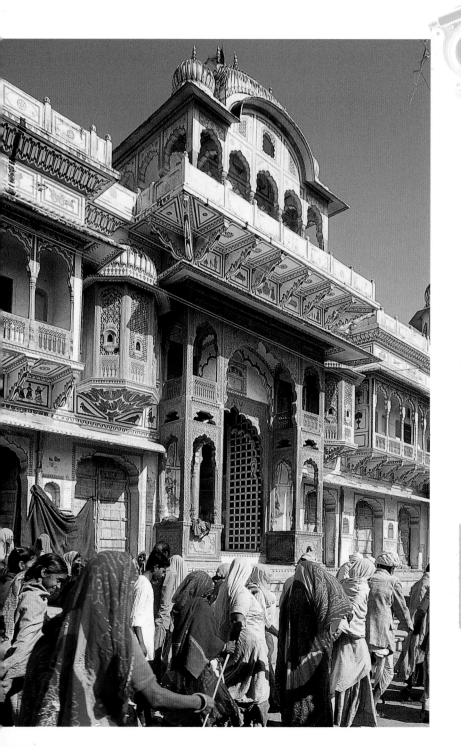

Seeing

Rajasthan must be one of the most **colourful** places on earth, I took this picture in the town of Pushkar, famous for its camel fair and for its **numerous temples**. I was struck by the way this particular temple was lit; from this **angle** the sunlight had created a very pleasing quality in the **stonework** with rich textures and bold colours.

Thinking

I wanted to show as much of the **building's facade** as possible but it was a narrow street and very busy so the **choice of viewpoint** was limited.

Acting

I found that from this position, using a **wide-angle lens**, I could include most of the temple's facade. This meant including some of the **people** in the foreground but I felt their colourful saris would add **impact** to the picture and also enhance the atmosphere of the place.

Rule of Thumb

When photographing buildings in city streets it's sometimes tempting to tilt the camera upwards to include the top. This should be done with care as it will result in the vertical lines of the building converging and giving the appearance of it toppling over. If you do tilt the camera, make sure it is done in a positive and deliberate way.

Towns & Cities

Seeing

The charming old town of Bruges in Belgium was the location for this picture of the small square of Walplein. I wanted to capture something of the leisurely atmosphere of the place with its horse-drawn carriages and pavement cafes.

Thinking

I walked around the square looking for a viewpoint which would allow me to include both the cafe tables and the row of old houses, which were lit very nicely by the early morning sunlight.

Acting

This spot seemed to achieve both aims. Although the cafe was mainly in shadow, this one table at the edge was well lit and I framed the image to include only this along with the buildings' facades in the background. I then waited until a carriage arrived in the street before shooting.

Technical Details
▼ 35mm SLR Camera with a 35–70mm zoom lens, an 81A warm-up filter and Fuji Provia.

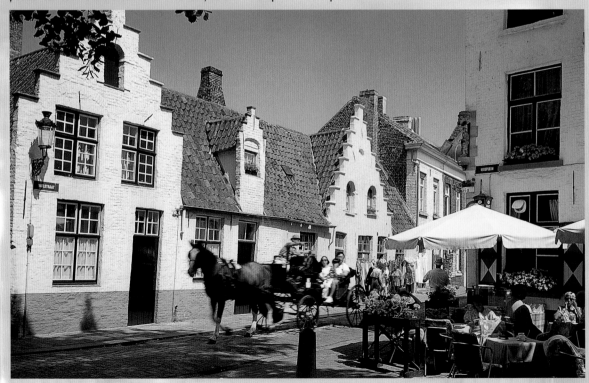

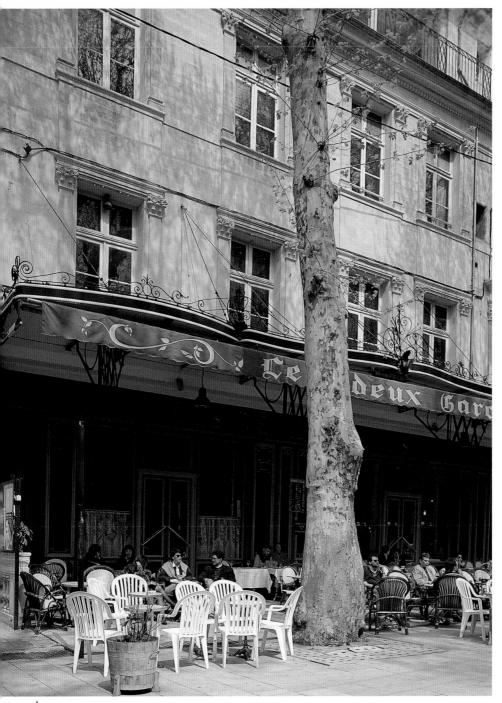

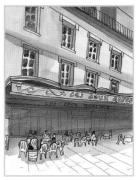

Aix-en-Provence is one of the most atmospheric cities in France known for its shady, tree-lined avenues and pavement cafes. This scene appealed to me because of the colour of the cafe's facade (one of Aix's best loved) and the dappled sunlight which was filtering through the trees. It was springtime so the foliage was not very dense and the sunlight was softened by the atmospheric haze, otherwise the effect might well have been too contrasty. I used a long-focus lens to isolate a small area of the scene from my viewpoint on the other side of the avenue, and framed the shot in a way that placed the plane tree about one third of the way across the image.

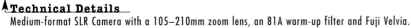

▲ Technical Details
Medium-format SLR Camera with a 105–210mm zoom lens, an 81A warm-up filter and Fuji Velvia.

Rule of Thumb

Taking photographs in busy cities is often made difficult because of the crowds of tourists who invariably throng the pavements and places of interest. It's well worth getting up a little early to avoid this as far fewer people will be around before breakfast and there is the added bonus of the low-angled sunlight providing a more pleasing and atmospheric light at an early hour.

Modern Architecture

Modern architecture is a dominant feature now of most large towns and cities no matter where you go in the world. Although buildings of concrete, steel and glass may lack the romantic appeal of ancient and historic buildings they do offer the photographer an opportunity to produce images with dramatic perspectives, bold patterns and a strong graphic quality.

Seeing

Looking up at these buildings towards the sun created a quite dramatic effect but it was a very contrasty scene and I could also see that the flare from the sun would be a problem.

Thinking

In order to maximise the perspective effect I decided to use my widest angle lens and shoot from a point almost immediately below the buildings so that I could tilt the camera up at a steep angle.

location
Los Angeles - USA

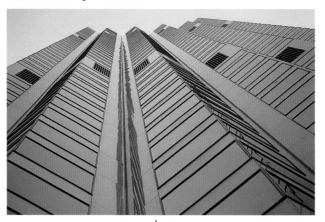

The use of pattern and perspective can be particularly effective in the context of modern architecture. Patterns can seem even bolder and perspective effects even more dramatic with pictures like this which have a limited colour range and soft lighting.

Technical Details
35mm Single Lens Reflex - 24mm lens, 81B warm-up filter, Kodachrome 64.

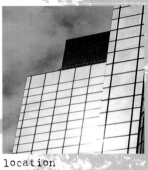

location
Cardiff, Wales - UK

A polarising filter is a very useful means of controlling the strength and brightness of reflections from non-metallic surfaces as in the glass facade of this office building.

location
Los Angeles - USA

Acting

I finely adjusted my viewpoint so the sun was partially obscured behind the building which reduced the amount of flare to an acceptable level. I also used a neutral graduated filter to further reduce the flare and to darken the top area of the sky.

Technique

The choice of viewpoint and the time of day are vital factors in determining the way a building is lit. From a particular viewpoint the light may only be angled satisfactorily at a certain time each day and it may be necessary to make several visits. For the most part of the day the front of this diner was in shadow and it was only in late afternoon when both elevations were illuminated. A compass can be a useful aid to estimating the best time to shoot from a specific viewpoint.

Technical Details
6x4.5cm Single Lens Reflex - 50mm perspective control lens, polarising and 81B warm-up filters, Fuji Velvia.

location
Roadside Diner - Massachussets, USA

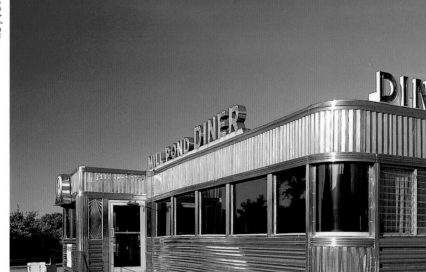

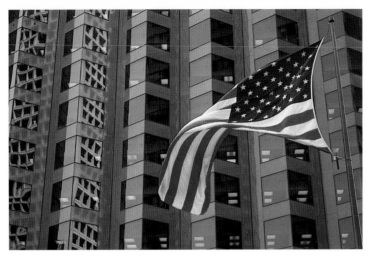

Rule of Thumb

Pattern alone is seldom completely satisfying and it is more effective if there is a detail or object within the pattern which breaks it and creates a focus of interest, like this flag fluttering in front of a high-rise building, for example.

location
San Francisco - USA

Rule of Thumb

Pattern is a visual element which invariably imparts an eye-catching quality when used in a composition. Modern buildings are usually a rich source of such images and often all that is needed to exploit them is a keen eye and a long-focus lens which allows you to isolate small sections of a structure.

location
San Francisco - USA

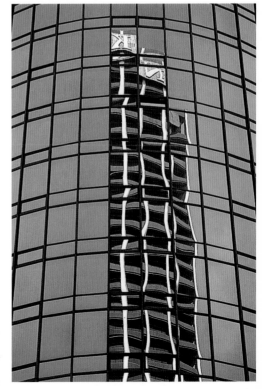

Technical Details
35mm Single Lens Reflex -
150mm lens, Kodachrome 64.

Technical Details
35mm Single Lens Reflex -
150mm lens, Kodachrome 64.

Trains, Boats & Planes

Travel is an almost inevitable part of a vacation. In some cases it is just something which has to be put up with in order to get to the destination, in other instances it is an integral part of the holiday, and, quite often, the journey itself is the main purpose of the trip. Whichever the case, a photograph or two which captures the experience of travelling invariably adds an interesting and valuable facet to a holiday record.

Seeing

I spotted this old Mississippi steam boat as it was about to leave the dock in New Orleans and realised I had little time to take my picture.

Thinking

I felt it would be more interesting to have some foreground interest rather than wait until the boat left the jetty and shoot it on its own, so I hurried as close as possible to the edge of the quay.

Acting

By using a wide-angle lens I was able to place part of the jetty and the wooden support posts in the close foreground which at the same time exaggerated the perspective of the boat and at the same time emphasised the churning paddle wheel.

Technical Details
▼ 35mm SLR Camera with a 20–35mm zoom lens, 81C warm-up and polarising filters, and Fuji Provia.

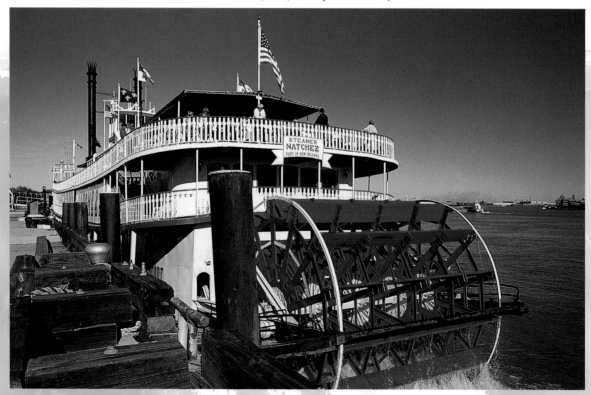

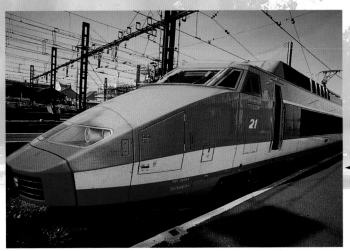

I took this photograph on a trip to Paris just after the French had introduced their TGV trains. It was late afternoon and the long shadows have contributed to the effect of the picture. I used a wide-angle lens from a very close viewpoint in order to exaggerate the perspective and to make the railway engine appear even more racy and aggressive. I framed the picture quite tightly to exclude some passengers who were visible further up the platform as I felt this would be distracting.

Technical Details
35mm SLR Camera with a 20–35mm zoom lens, an 81A warm-up filter and Fuji Velvia.

Technical Details
35mm SLR Camera with a 24–85mm zoom lens, an 81B warm-up filter and Kodak Ektachrome 100 SW.

I was lucky to get a window seat on the best side of the plane on this occasion, i.e. facing away from the sun. I used a wide-angle lens and placed it as close to the glass as possible without touching it, and I used my fastest shutter speed. I also fitted an 81B warm-up filter to counter the strong blue cast which is created by UV light at high altitudes.

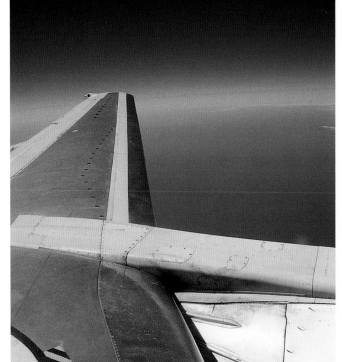

Rule of Thumb

When shooting pictures from a moving vehicle it's wise to use the fastest shutter speed which conditions will allow. It can help to pan the camera with the movement, holding your subject as steady in the frame as possible. But do resist the temptation to brace the camera against a window, when in a plane, for example, as the engine vibration can cause noticeable image blurring.

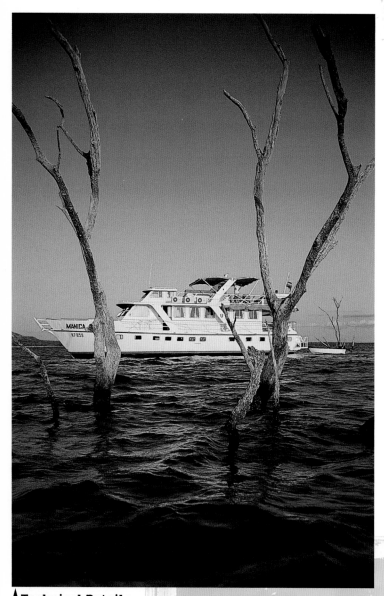

Seeing

I'd spent several days on this boat travelling along the shores of Lake Kariba in Zimbabwe. I wanted to have a picture of the boat but, again, most of the opportunities had been in the middle of the day and the results had lacked that dramatic edge.

Thinking

On this occasion we had moored close to some of the drowned trees which were a feature of the man-made lake and I thought I might be able to use some of these in the shot.

Acting

I thought my best chance would be to shoot at first light when the sun was low in the sky and asked the skipper if he would ferry me out in the dinghy to take my shots. I soon found this viewpoint where I could frame the boat between two trees and also have a nice glancing light on the side of the boat together with a strong reflection in the water.

Technical Tip

A neutral-graduated filter will invariably improve the quality and effect of sunset shots. It enables you to give more exposure to darker foreground details without over-exposing the sky and losing its rich colour and tone.

Technical Details

35mm SLR Camera with a 75–300mm zoom lens, an 81A warm-up filter and Fuji Velvia.

The Kent and East Sussex railway in the UK was the location of this shot where the pleasure of travelling on a real old steam engine can still be enjoyed, albeit for a fairly short journey. This picture was taken at its terminal station in Tenterden and my viewpoint was from the road bridge crossing the line, using a long-focus lens. Shooting into the light has shown up the steam quite well and I liked the guard's leisurely pose.

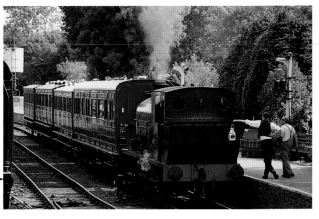

Technical Details
35mm SLR Camera with a 35–70mm zoom lens and Fuji Provia.

A Mississippi river-boat cruise was the occasion for this picture which was taken at the town of Natchez where we'd stopped for a shore excursion. I was keen to have a nice shot of the paddle boat I'd spent the week on but until now the opportunities had all been in the middle of the day and had lacked atmosphere. On this occasion we'd returned late to the boat and the sun had just set enabling me to shoot this picture fairly quickly before boarding. I was lucky not only to have such a good sky but also that the boat had been moored in front of the bridge.

Technical Details
▼35mm SLR Camera with a 35–70mm zoom lens, a neutral-graduated filter and Fuji Velvia.

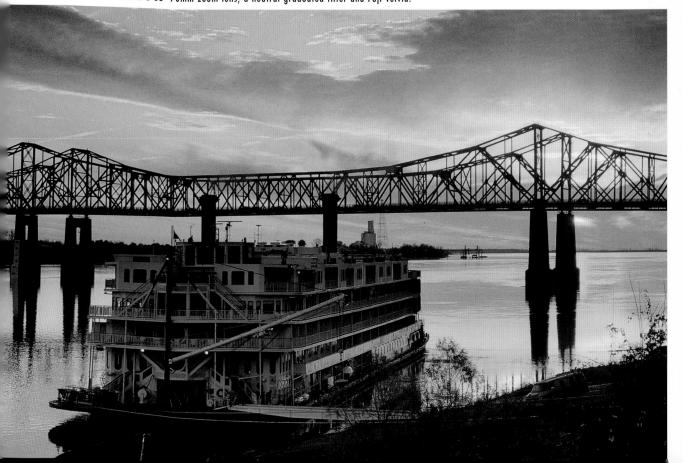

Photographing Interiors

Taking photographs of interiors is something a travel photographer sometimes needs to do and they can often prove to be more interesting and photogenic than exterior shots. But such pictures can present a number of special problems. A great deal depends upon the way the space is lit. Many buildings, like churches and cathedrals for instance, have what seems to be a very dimly lit interior, often with just the natural daylight which filters through the windows. Providing this is fairly evenly distributed, the low level of illumination need not be a problem, as a camera mounted on a tripod can be given as long an exposure as necessary.

Seeing

The alter piece was the obvious focus point in this interior and I thought it would be most effective to place it in the centre of the image and go for a symmetrical composition.

Thinking

The church was lit by a mixture of daylight from the windows and artificial light. Although I thought the latter would probably be dominant I opted for daylight film as I would prefer the shot to have a warm quality rather than a bluish one.

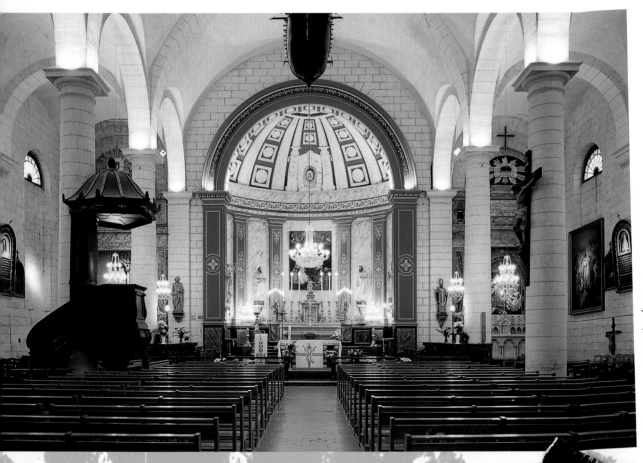

location
La Mezquita - Cordoba - Andalucia, Spain

Acting

I used a **perspective control** lens as the foreground lacked interest and I did not want to tilt the camera and have **converging** verticals. I fitted a blue 82B filter to prevent the artificial light from creating an excessively strong orange cast on the daylight film.

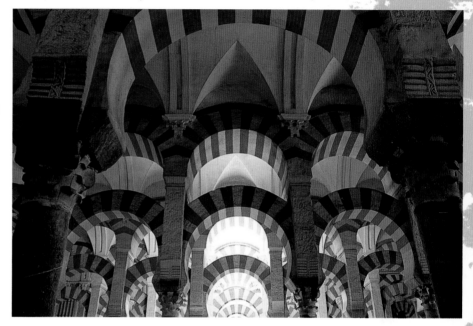

Rule of Thumb

A good way of judging just how evenly, or otherwise, the space is lit to view the scene through half-closed eyes, this will readily show if there is a big difference between the lighter and darker areas of the interior. Alternatively you can view the subject through the camera with the lens stopped down using the depth-of-field preview button.

Technical Details ➤
35mm Single Lens Reflex - 28mm perspective control lens, 82B filter, 12secs at f8, Kodak Ektachrome E100S.

◄ **Technical Details**
35mm Single Lens Reflex - 35-70mm zoom lens, 2 secs at f5.6, Fuji Provia.

Seeing

It was the vastness of this interior, photographed from a first floor gallery, which first impressed me but the mass of brokers filling the floor was equally striking.

Thinking

My first thought, and action, was to shoot on a wide-angle lens using horizontal format. But the most crowded part of the floor was in the centre and the impact of the mass of people seemed greater if I framed the image more tightly.

Acting

I switched to a lens with a narrower field of view and changed to an upright format in order to exclude the less crowded edges of the image. As the interior lighting was of a completely unknown quality I opted to use daylight film with no filter but the resulting image has a greenish cast which, in retrospect, I would have preferred to have corrected.

Technique

When a subject is lit by predominately fluorescent lighting it is best to shoot on daylight film using a magenta tinted filter. The strength of the filter needed depends upon the precise nature of the fluorescent tube but a fairly safe bet is to use an FLD conversion filter.

location
Stock Exchange - Tokyo, Japan

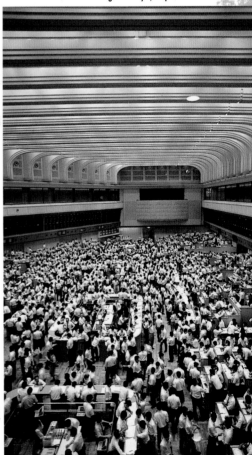

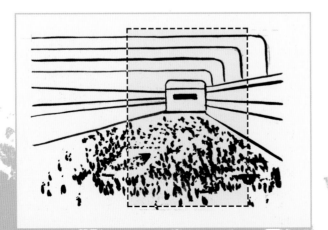

Technical Details
35mm Single Lens Reflex - 35mm lens,
1 sec at f5.6, Kodak High Speed Ektachrome.

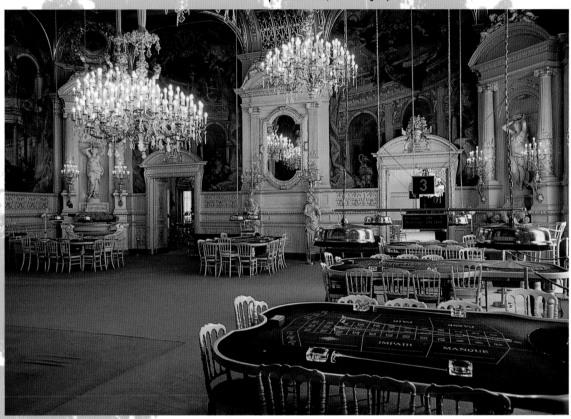

location
The Casino, Baden Baden - Germany

◄ **Technical Details**
35mm Single Lens Reflex - 35mm lens, 1/4
sec at 14, High Speed Ektachrome.

Rule of Thumb

When confronted with mixed
lighting, or lighting of an
unknown colour quality it is
safer to shoot on colour
negative film as this is more
tolerant of colour temperature
variations and the image can
be easily corrected at the
printing stage.

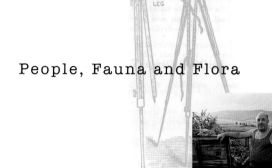

People, Fauna and Flora

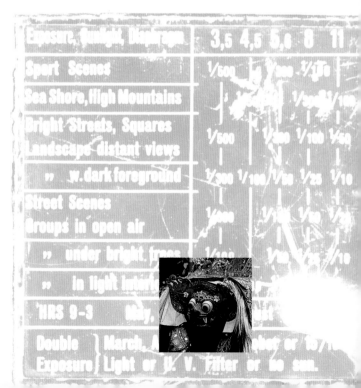

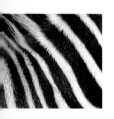

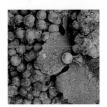

There are some situations that obviously demand a
special approach – shooting on safari, for example. However, there are other occasions that
also require careful thought and which you may not have considered before, such as shooting
in crowded places, dealing with close-ups or shooting photo
essays. Find out how to approach all these and more.

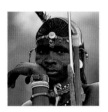

2

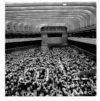

Photographing People

If you watch the prints being discharged from a one-hour photolab it's pretty evident that a high proportion of the photographs taken during a vacation are of people and the majority of these are of the participants themselves. It's quite natural that you should want to have a record of yourself and your partner or companions during a holiday break but it's a shame to let this dominate a collection of photographs. It can only add to the pleasure of a holiday record if you also photograph people you meet, local characters and anyone who has contributed to your holiday experience.

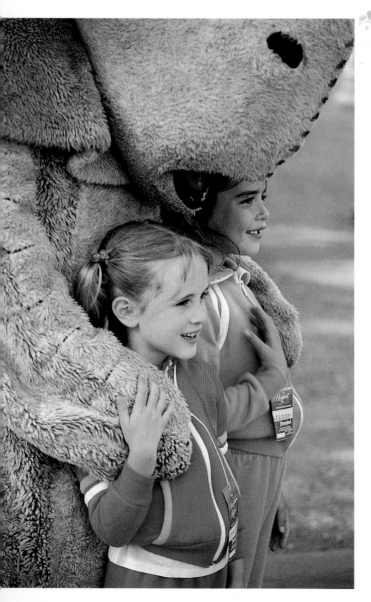

Seeing

I spotted these two young girls during a visit to Disneyland and watched as they had their photograph taken as they posed with one of the costumed characters. The scene appealed to me partly because of the pleasing colours – soft blues, greys and pinks – as much as because of the situation itself.

Thinking

I wanted to find a way of making my picture different to the "stand and smile" shot I would have got if I'd shot it from where their parents were taking their picture.

Acting

I found that by standing to the side I could see both of their expressions clearly and, at the same time, was able to use the Disney character as a frame to the image, creating a nicely compact composition. It also produced a more spontaneous, less posed effect.

◄ Technical Details
35mm SLR Camera with a 75–300mm zoom lens, an 81A warm-up filter and Kodachrome 64.

This rather glum little girl was having her face painted at a village fete and I could not resist the contrast between the seriousness of her expression and the appearance of her face. I framed the image very tightly using a long-focus lens to focus attention on her features.

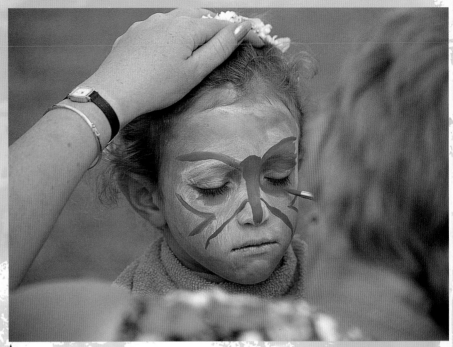

↑Technical Details
35mm SLR Camera with a 70–200mm zoom lens, an 81A warm-up filter and Fuji Provia.

Technical Details
▼35mm SLR Camera with a 75–300mm zoom lens, an 81A warm-up filter and Fuji Provia.

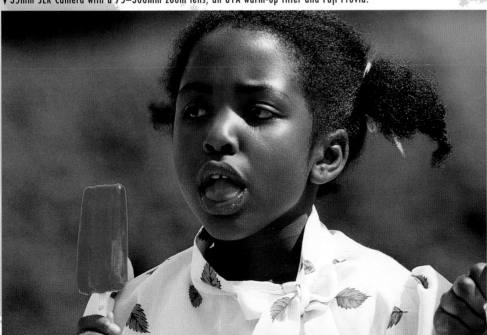

This little girl was enjoying herself at the Nairobi races in Kenya and I was taken with the contrast between her ice lolly and the rest of the image. I was in the process of framing the shot tightly using a long-focus lens when she suddenly poked out a red tongue which was just the icing on the cake for this shot.

Photographing People

Seeing

This Bedouin had been a guide on a photographic workshop I was accompanying. On this occasion, he had organised a **photo opportunity** in which the participants were able to shoot him and a friend riding their camels **over the dunes** in southern Morocco.

Thinking

This had provided some **good moments** but the early morning light was very **soft and hazy** resulting in the more distant shots being rather flat and **lacking in sparkle**. Because of this I thought that perhaps a more **conventional portrait** might produce a better picture.

Acting

I asked him to sit close to his camel on the **sand** with his back to the sun and in a spot where the dune **behind him** would provide a plain, **uncluttered background**. I framed the image to include all of him and enough of his companion to **balance** the composition.

Technical Details
35mm SLR Camera with a 75–200mm zoom lens, an 81A warm-up filter and Fuji Provia.

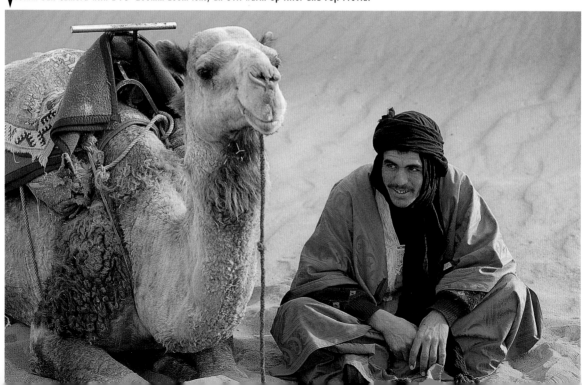

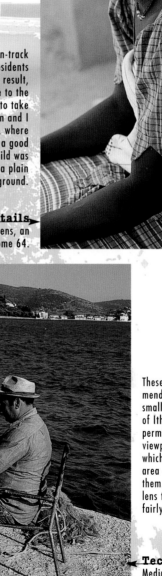

I'd had the opportunity to visit an off-the-beaten-track village in the Gambia, West Africa, where the residents were not at all accustomed to tourists, and, as a result, had a very natural and relaxed attitude to the occasional visitor like myself. This allowed me to take pictures of the villagers with their cooperation and I was able to ask them to sit in a particular spot, where the light was pleasing and there was a good background. This portrait of a mother and child was shot in open shade with soft lighting and I used a plain wall as a contrasting background.

Technical Details
35mm SLR Camera with a 75–300mm zoom lens, an 81A warm-up filter and Kodachrome 64.

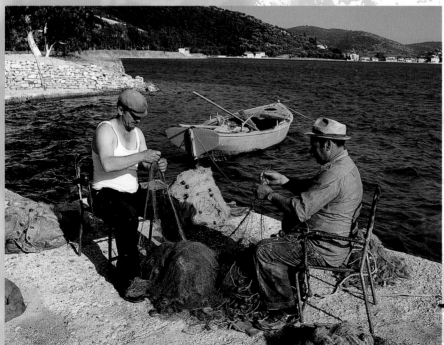

These two fishermen were mending their nets beside a small bay in the Greek island of Ithaca. After asking their permission I simply chose a viewpoint quite close to them which placed the most scenic area of the background behind them. I then used a wide-angle lens to enable me to include a fairly wide expanse of this.

Technical Details
Medium-format SLR Camera with a 55mm wide-angle lens, 81C warm-up and polarising filters, and Kodak Ektachrome 64.

Photographing People

Seeing

The village of Montehermosa in Spain's Extramadura region is known for its unique handicrafts which have a very South American look, probably as a result of returning Conquistadors. I wanted to photograph one of the ladies wearing her traditional costume, who was selling her handicrafts from a roadside stall.

Thinking

But shooting in this setting was almost impossible as the sunlight was harsh and contrasty and both the surroundings and background very untidy and distracting.

Acting

I asked the lady if she would mind moving over near the wall of a house which was in shade. This provided a much softer and more pleasing light and I was also able to use it as a less cluttered and more unobtrusive background. The illustration shows how the image would have been too cluttered and the subject less defined had a plain, contrasting background not been used.

Technical Details

▼ 35mm SLR Camera with a 20–35mm zoom lens, an 81A warm-up filter and Fuji Provia.

The streets of old Delhi in India are the home of this small family. I was a bit doubtful about approaching them for a picture as I was keen to avoid intruding on their privacy and my presence could, very understandably, cause a somewhat resentful response. But my tentative request was met with amusement, interest and even enthusiasm. Using a wide-angle lens I simply framed the image in a way that included all of the family but excluded as many of the extraneous details as possible.

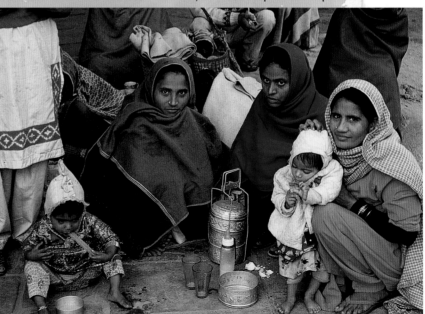

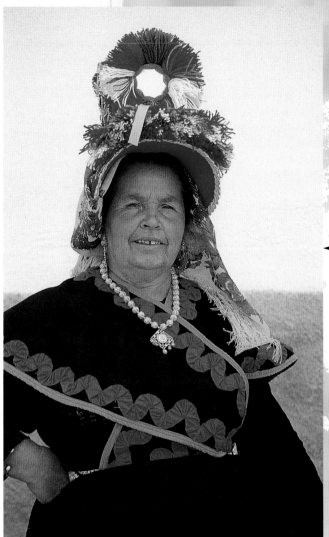

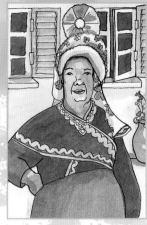

Technical Details
35mm SLR Camera with a 35–70mm zoom lens, an 81A
warm-up filter and Fuji Velvia.

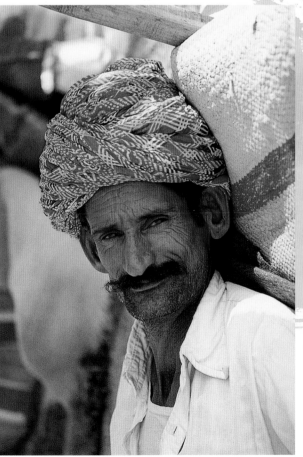

This very relaxed gentleman was taking a rest during the
Pushkar Camel fair in India. Rajastahni tribesmen take
considerable pride in their appearance, and, in my
experience, really love to be photographed. In spite of
having his rest disturbed, this man was ready and willing
with a smile when he saw my raised camera. Using a
long-focus lens, I simply framed the image tightly to
concentrate attention on his strong features.

Technical Details
35mm SLR Camera with a 75–300mm zoom lens, an
81A warm-up filter and Fuji Provia.

Informal Portraits

While taking shots of people while they are unaware of the camera can produce spontaneous and natural images there are occasions when it can be better to ask their permission and have your subject's cooperation. Before you do so, think about the best place to place them and how they should be posed as you will then be able to work more positively and quickly which helps to make your subject more at ease.

Seeing

I saw this marvellous character loading his cart as I drove past and felt he would make a great subject, especially as the background was also ideal and would contribute to the atmosphere and composition of the shot.

location
Alsace - France

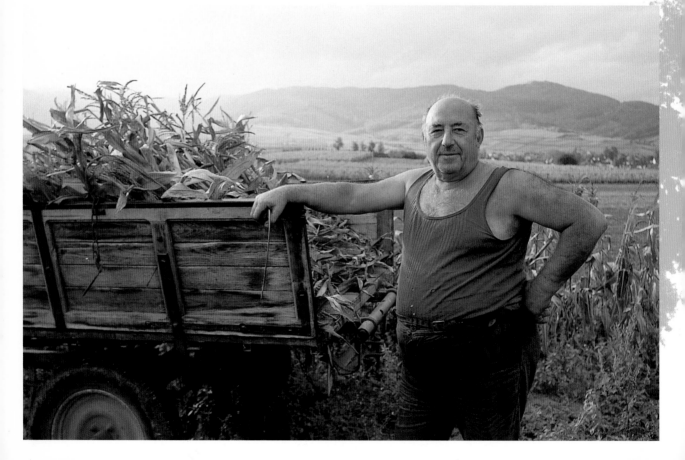

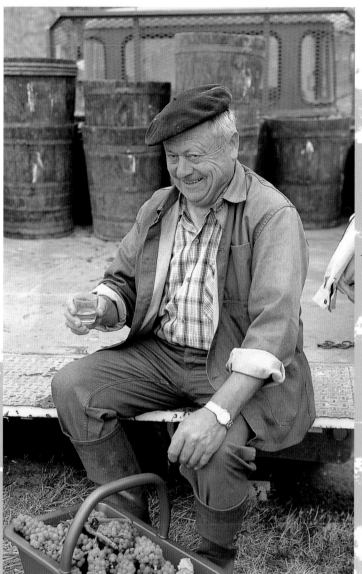

Technique

Having your subject seated tends to be best for portraits in general - on a wall, tree trunk or even on the ground is preferable to standing. It can help when the model is able to sit in such a way that he or she can lean forward to support arms or elbows on something as this makes for a more relaxed and natural picture.

◄ Technical Details
35mm Single Lens Reflex -
35-70mm zoom lens - Fuji Provia.

Thinking

It was obvious I needed to ask permission as he had already noticed me stop and was doubtless wondering what I wanted. I felt I might as well go a stage further and ask him to take up a position beside the cart - he was very happy to oblige.

Acting

Placing his arm on the cart linked the two elements together very well and also helped him to feel more relaxed. I used a wide-angle lens so that I could get quite close to him but, at the same time include enough of the background and cart to establish the setting.

location
Muscadet Vineyards - Loire, France

◄ Technical Details
35mm Single Lens Reflex - 35-
70mm zoom lens, Fuji Velvia.

Technical Details
35mm Single Lens Reflex -
80-200mm zoom lens, Fuji Provia.

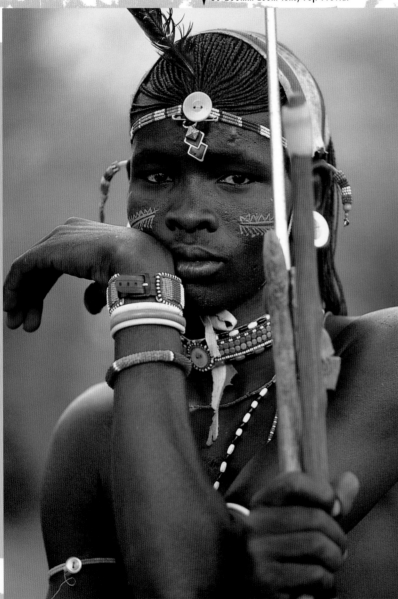

location
Samburu Tribesman - Kenya

Seeing

I saw this handsome man among a group of dancers in a Samburu village and felt he would make a good subject for a striking portrait. It was a bright sunny day making the colours and textures of the scene became rather confused and distracting.

I shot this full-length portrait on a long-focus lens using a fairly distant viewpoint so that I could select a small area of the scene to act as a background as well as creating a more interesting perspective.

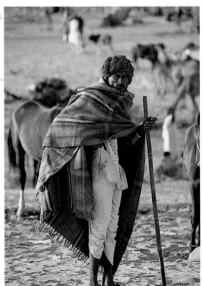

location
Pushkar Camel Fair - Rajasthan, India

Thinking

There was a group of trees to one side of the area where the dancers were performing and I thought the shade they provided would create a more pleasing lighting quality for a head-and-shoulder portrait.

Acting

I picked out a spot where the background was fairly unobtrusive and waited until the performance had ended before approaching my subject. I asked him to move into the spot I'd picked and suggested he lean on his spear to create a nice shape and make him appear relaxed. I used a long-focus lens to frame the image quite tightly and set a wide aperture to ensure the background details were out of focus.

Technique

Direct sunlight can often create an unattractive quality with portraits and shooting into the light, with the sun behind the subject, is often a better option. But it does need some care. It is important to ensure that the sunlight does not fall directly upon the lens as this can cause flare and degrade the image. It's also necessary to increase the exposure indicated by an average reading, or to take a close-up or spot reading from a mid tone within the subject.

Technical Details
35mm Single Lens Reflex - 75-300mm zoom lens, 1/500 sec at f5.6, Fuji Provia.

Technical Details
35mm Single Lens Reflex - 35mm lens, Fuji Provia.

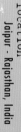

location
Jaipur - Rajasthan, India

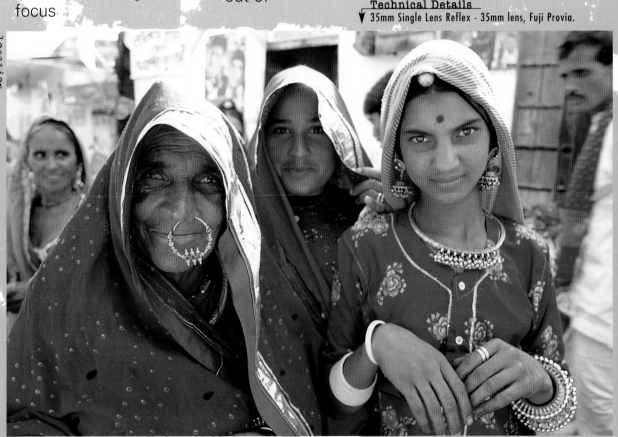

Shooting Unobserved

Photographing people when they are unaware of the camera can be an important and very effective part of travel photography but is also one of the most difficult things to do successfully, especially when working in an alien culture where the presence of a stranger can be a noteworthy event. This type of photography is easiest to achieve when your subjects are preoccupied with some activity and surrounded by others, such as at a market or in a busy street.

Seeing

This lady seemed to be an ideal subject because she was nicely posed against a plain, uncluttered background and the pile of baskets added interest and balance to the composition.

Thinking

As I did not want to shoot her looking into the camera I chose my viewpoint so she was nicely placed against the background and then directed my attention away from her pretending to shoot pictures elsewhere.

location
Street Market - Bali

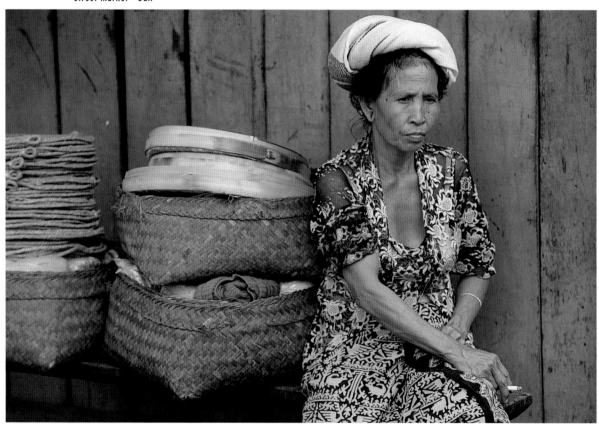

A zoom lens is very useful for shots like this as you can adjust the way the image is framed without having to change you viewpoint and risk attracting your subject's attention.

Rule of Thumb

If you get caught redhanded trying to shoot a candid of someone it's far better to just smile and say, or mime "I hope you don't mind" than to turn away. Few people will be offended if you use a little charm and you can often get the chance to shoot another picture with their cooperation.

Acting

The moment her interest in me waned and she became **preoccupied** with other things I quickly **re-aimed** the camera and made my exposures, having **preset** the exposure and focussing.

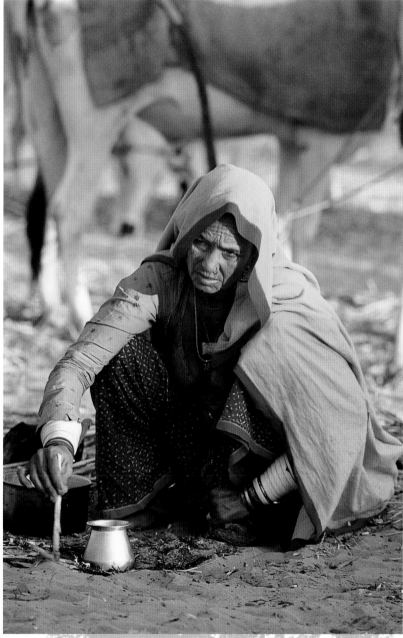

location
Pushkar Camel Fair - Rajasthan, India

Technical Details
35mm Single Lens Reflex - 105mm lens, Fuji Provia.

Technical Details
35mm Single Lens Reflex - 70-210mm lens, Fuji Provia.

People in their Environment

While photographing subjects like the countryside, famous landmarks and historic buildings is a very important aspect of travel photography, and one which is very effective in establishing the identity of a location, it's also necessary to show something of the life and character of a country's population in order to show a full picture of a particular destination.

Rule of Thumb

When you want to photograph people within a setting, a wide-angle lens will allow you to get quite close to your subject and still include a large area of the background. But you do need to choose a viewpoint and frame the image carefully to ensure the composition is well balanced and there are no conflicting details.

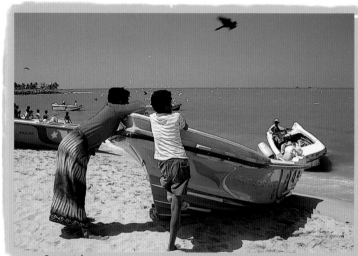

location
Negombo - Sri Lanka

Technical Details
35mm Single Lens Reflex - 35mm lens polarising and 81C warm-up filters, Fuji Velvia.

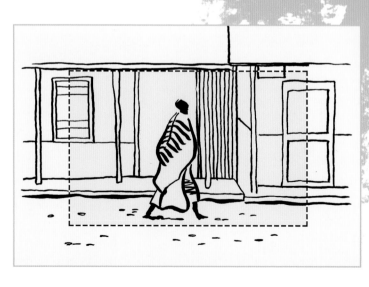

Seeing

This scene, of a Masai village, was a very colourful situation with many people jostling around a small square in front of a row of shanty-town shops. There was strong overhead sunlight which tended to make the vividly dressed Masai become an unmanageable jumble of colour and detail.

Technical Details
35mm Single Lens Reflex - 80-200mm zoom lens, 81A warm-up filter, Fuji Provia.

location

Amboseli
- Kenya

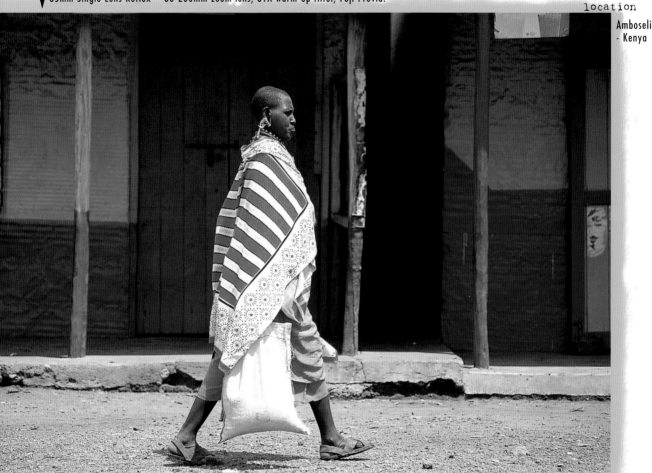

Thinking

Because of this I decided to use a fairly **distant** viewpoint with a long-focus lens to **isolate** small areas of the scene and to enable me to focus attention on various individuals instead of attempting to record a wider view.

Acting

I chose a **viewpoint** and framed the image so that a dark and fairly **featureless** area of the scene acted as a **background** and then simply waited until a suitable subject moved into the right position.

One of the pleasures of travelling is that of encountering local events such as festivals, folk customs and street parades. Successful photography of occasions like these depend a great deal upon securing a good vantage point. At these events you will benefit enormously from an early arrival and good reconnaissance. It also helps to talk to officials in order to discover where the best positions might be and when the most exciting parts of the proceedings will take place.

Seeing

The action is of course the main point of a shot like this but I also wanted to capture something of the setting and atmosphere of the occasion.

Thinking

This particular event meant that the most dramatic part of the action took place at a fairly predictable point - where the horse was first released from its pen - and it often lasted for only a few seconds before the cowboy was removed.

Acting

I walked around the edge of the arena looking for a viewpoint where I had a clear view of the horse emerging but also was able to include a little of the setting itself.

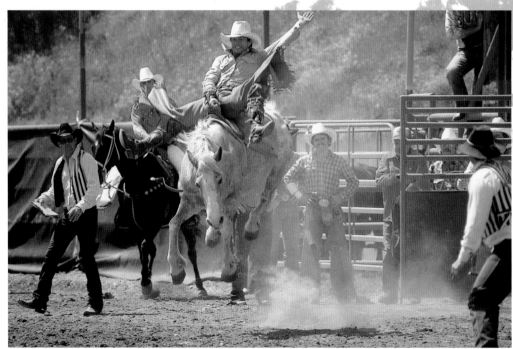

location
Rodeo, California - USA

Technical Details
6x4.5cm Single Lens Reflex - 105mm lens,
125 sec at f4,
Fuji Provia rated at ISO 200.

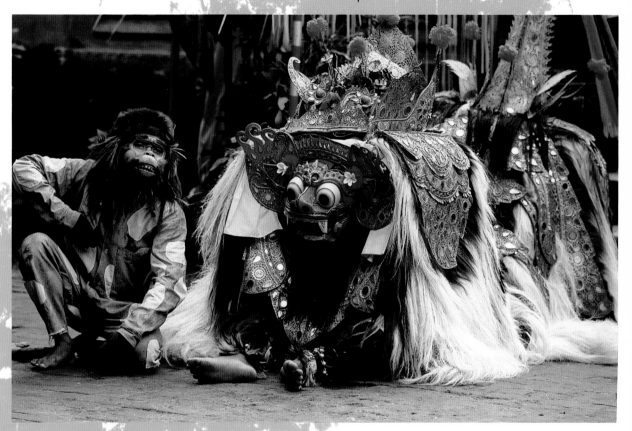

location
Traditional Theatre - Bali

Technical Details
35mm Single Lens Reflex -
300mm lens,
1/500 sec at f5.6,
Kodak High Speed
Ektachrome.

Technique

When shooting in low light and a fast shutter speed is needed it is possible to rate the film at one or two stops faster than its stated speed and to ask the processing laboratory to push process the film by one or two stops respectively.

Events & Occasions

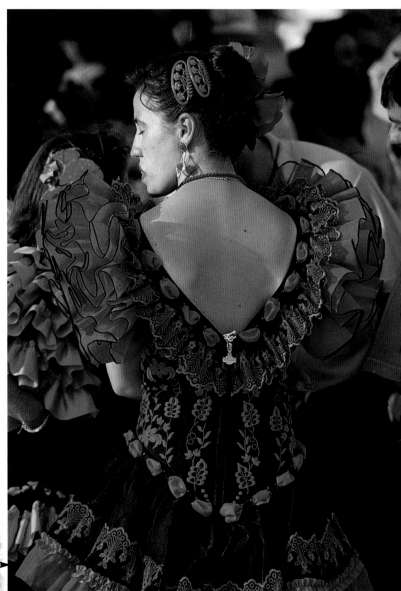

Seeing

I had discovered that a small local festival was taking place at a village near where I was staying in the Andalucia region of Spain and decided to go and have a look. It was very colourful and the villagers had taken a great deal of trouble, dressing up in their finest traditional costumes, and decorating their horse and ox carts.

Thinking

The event was taking place on a large area of waste ground some distance away from the village. It was littered by parked cars and the whole scene was very untidy.

Acting

I made several attempts to shoot a wider view of the situation but there was always something distracting and intrusive in the background. In the end I decided to fit a long-focus lens on my camera and simply look for evocative details. This close-up of a glamourous flamenco dress was one of them.

Technical Details
35mm SLR Camera with a 75–300mm zoom lens, an 81A warm-up filter and Fuji Provia.

Rule of Thumb

It's always a good idea to visit the local tourist office, town hall or information centre at your holiday destination to discover what events may be taking place during your visit. As well as the bigger annual events, more modest affairs, like a weekly market, can also be good hunting grounds for photographs and will add some good local colour to your collection of pictures.

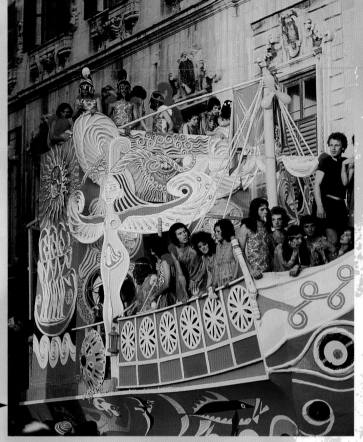

A street parade in the Maltese capital of Valetta provided this opportunity. I had managed to push myself to the front of the crowd for an unobstructed viewpoint which gave me a sympathetic background, and then waited until an interesting float passed by. The shot was taken very late in the day as the sun was going down which has created this rather nice, warm atmospheric lighting.

Technical Details
35mm SLR Camera with a 35–70mm zoom lens, an 81A warm-up filter and Kodak Ektachrome 64.

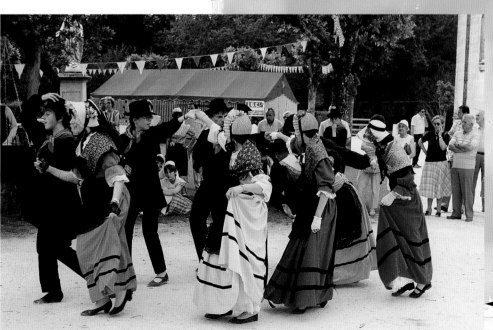

A wine fair in a French village was going on when I drove through. It was quite unexpected and because it was a small local event with no big crowds it was relatively easy to move around freely looking for pictures. I watched this group of costumed dancers for a while and looked for a viewpoint which would give me an interesting, but not too distracting background. I used a long-focus lens to enlarge the group within the frame from a distant viewpoint and to crop out unwanted details.

Technical Details
35mm SLR Camera with a 75–300mm zoom lens, an 81A warm-up filter and Fuji Provia.

Photography on Safari

Taking photographs while on safari is quite different to most other types of photography and needs a rather different approach as well as the use of different techniques. Within the national game parks, where most safari trips take place, it is generally forbidden to leave the vehicle and this in itself requires a fairly radical change to the way photographs are normally taken. Choosing a viewpoint is largely a question of ensuring the vehicle is in the right place and you are in the best position within it.

Seeing

This young zebra had a very obvious **appeal** and it's closeness to its parent suggested there might be a way of photographing them together.

Thinking

I felt a very **tightly framed** shot would give the image additional impact and would also emphasise the striking **pattern** create by their striped bodies.

location
Young Zebra, Masai Mara - Kenya

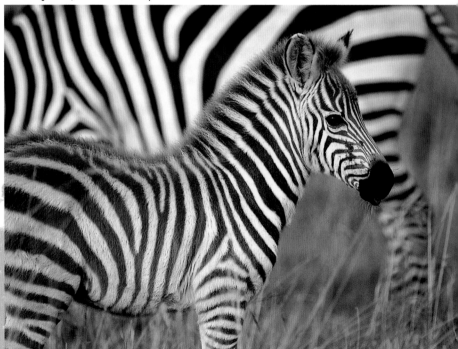

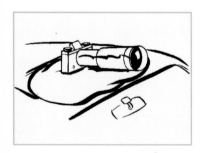

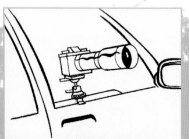

When using long focus lenses it is vital to have some form of support to avoid the risk of camera shake. In a vehicle a bean bag rested on the window frame or roof hatch is ideal. Alternatively, you can buy a bracket which clamps onto the window and a monopod is also a useful form of support when a tripod can't be used.

Acting

I asked the Landrover driver to get as close as he could and fitted the 600mm lens to give me a very close-up image. It was also necessary to drive very slowly and quietly to one side of the zebras to obtain the most effective juxtaposition between their two bodies.

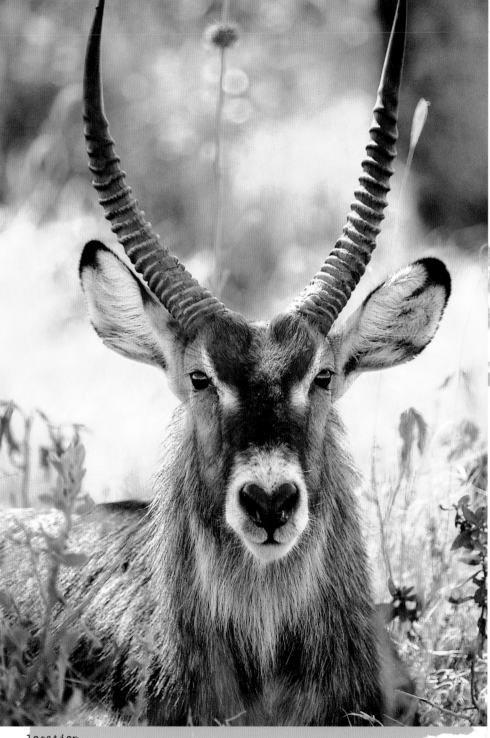

◄ **Technical Details**
35mm Single Lens Reflex - 600mm lens, 1/500 sec at f4, Fuji Provia.

Technical Details ►
35mm Single Lens Reflex - 600mm lens, 1/250 sec at f4, Fuji Provia.

location
Waterbuck - Nakuru, Kenya

Rule of Thumb

Where possible, try to set the subject against a fairly plain, contrasting tone or colour and avoid the presence of distracting highlights or details behind the animal or bird.

Seeing

The bold markings of this giraffe were emphasised by the warm colour of the sunlight in the late afternoon and as the animal was on the move I felt it might produce a strong image.

Thinking

I asked the driver to move slowly ahead of the animal until I found an area of fairly plain background across which I thought it would travel.

Acting

I followed the animal in my viewfinder as it approached, keeping it in focus and waiting until it moved into the best position before making my exposures. It was just a happy chance that, at this moment, the giraffe leaned forward to create this nice shape.

Technical Details ➤
35mm Single Lens Reflex - 600mm lens, 1/500 sec at f4, Fuji Provia.

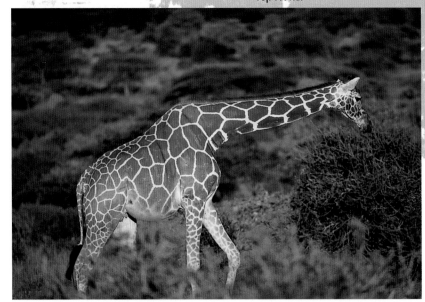

location
Reticulated
Giraffe -
Samburu,
Kenya

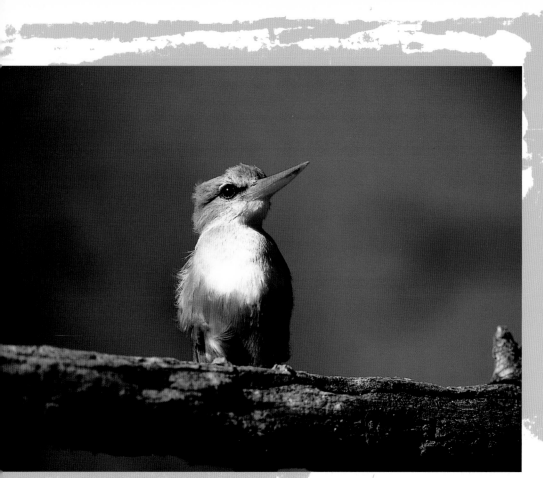

location
Kingfisher - Samburu, Kenya

Technique

Getting close enough to your subject is the first concern when choosing a viewpoint but it's also necessary to consider the lighting. In bright sunlight the contrast can easily create an unattractive quality in photographs with dense shadows and burned out highlights and the choice of viewpoint can be a vital factor if this problem is to be avoided.

Technical Details
35mm Single Lens Reflex -
150-500mm zoom lens,
1/250 sec at f5.6, Fuji Provia.

Trees & Plants

The photography of local flora is something which needs a rather different approach to most general travel subjects but is an effective way of adding an extra dimension to the coverage of a region as well as providing both variety and interest to a collection of photographs. In many cases, shots of this type can do a great deal towards helping to create a sense of place and in conveying the character and atmosphere of a particular country.

Rule of Thumb

When photographing blooms and foliage you will find that a polarising filter will often increase the colour saturation considerably and in some cases, as in this shot of Bougainvillia, help to render a difficult colour more accurately.

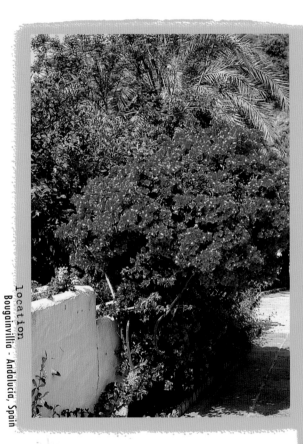

location
Bougainvillia - Andalucia, Spain

Seeing

Late evening sunlight illuminated this Acacia tree from the side throwing its skeletal branches into stark relief and a dark stormy sky behind gave it additional impact and drama.

Thinking

I felt the picture would be most effective if I could isolate the tree as much as possible from its surroundings and frame it tightly to emphasise the bold shapes created by its trunks and branches.

Acting

I found a viewpoint from which there was a clear gap between the trees on each side of my subject and used a long-focus lens to exclude them from the frame. I gave a half stop exposure less than indicated to maximise the contrast between the dark sky and the brightly lit tree.

Technical Details
35mm Single Lens Reflex - 35-70mm zoom lens, polarising and 81B warm-up filters, Fuji Velvia.

Technical Details
35mm Single Lens Reflex - 80-200mm zoom lens, 81C warm-up filter, Fuji Provia.

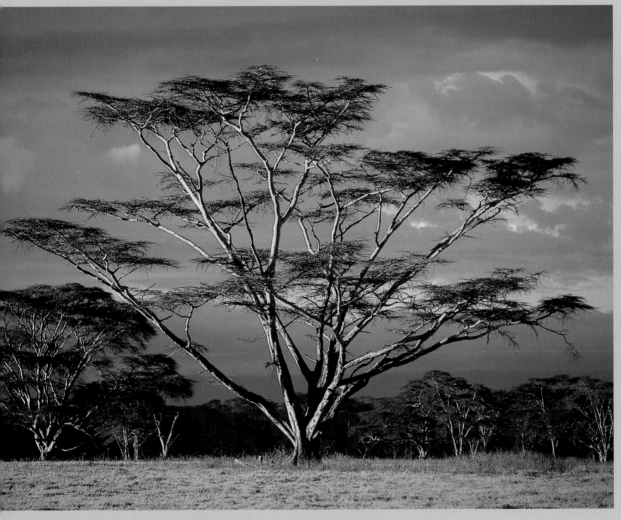

location
Acacia Tree - Nakuru, Kenya

location
Spring Crocus, Wensleydale - Yorkshire, UK

Technical Details
35mm Single Lens Reflex - 75-150mm zoom
lens, extension tube, Fuji Velvia.

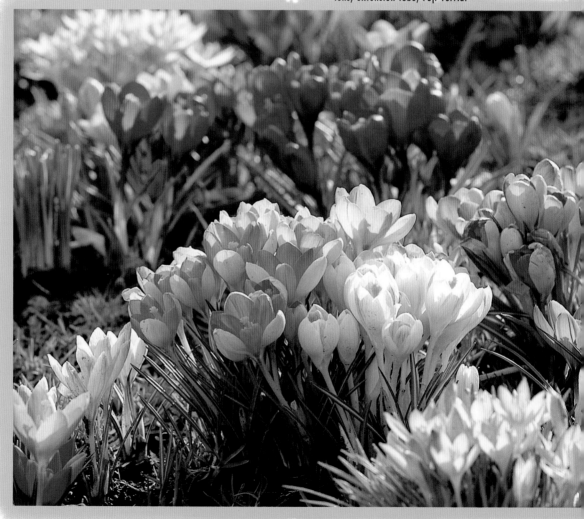

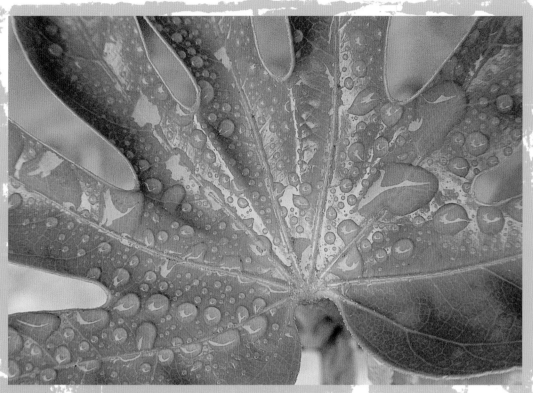

location
Fig Plant - Sri Lanka

Technique

When a subject has a bold or interesting texture, like this leaf with water droplets, it can be very effective to get really close to the subject in order to reveal the very smallest details. But at this degree of close-up the slightest camera movement with cause the image to become blurred and it is necessary to use a tripod.

Rule of Thumb

The bright sunlight in this shot created high contrast with bright highlights and dense shadows which are best avoided for colourful close-up photographs. In these situations, shooting against the light will often produce a more pleasing quality.

Technical Details
6x4.5cm Single Lens Reflex - 105-210 zoom lens, extension tube, 1/8 sec @ f16, Fuji Velvia.

Close-up Photography

With the majority of photographs, the lens is focussed at a distance of two metres or more but when a closer view of a subject is needed, and the focussing distance is significantly closer than this, there are a number of special considerations to be made. One metre or so is the usual close-focussing limit of normal lenses but there are several ways of reducing this limit. Many ordinary zoom lenses now have a macro setting which will allow it to be focussed down to a few inches but this is often only at one setting of the zoom's focal length.

Seeing

These grapes have developed "noble rot" an important stage in the production of the famous sweet desert wine, Monbazillac. It was necessary to use a very close-up image in order to show the appearance of the fruit.

Thinking

I felt a very straightforward approach would be best and that a flat on shot of the grapes in their trug would show the texture and colour most effectively.

Acting

I moved the trug into the shade to ensure the lighting was soft and there were no strong shadows or bright highlights and set my tripod so I could aim the camera straight down onto the grapes. I placed a few vine leaves to add interest to the composition and set a small aperture to ensure adequate depth of field.

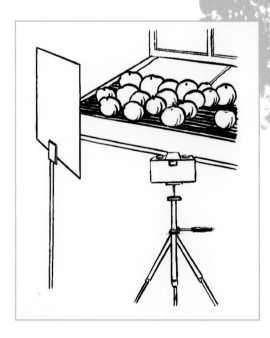

Technique

Lighting quality is an important factor with many close-up subjects, as subtleties of colour and texture can easily be obscured by areas of shadow. With close ups, like this shot of fruit, it's a simple matter to use a reflector or fill-in flash to throw light into the shadows.

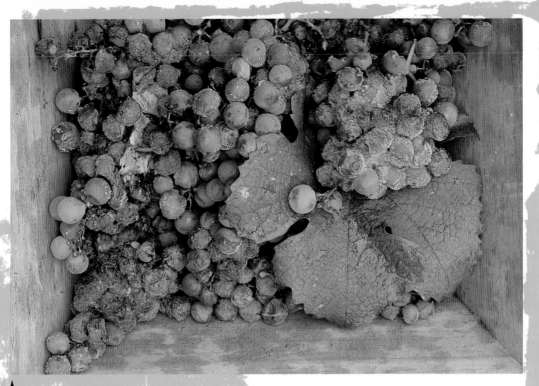

location
The Vineyards
of Monbazillac,
near Bergerac
- Dordogne,
France

Technical Details
35mm Single Lens Reflex -
35-70mm zoom lens, extension tube,
1/4 sec at f16, Fuji Velvia.

location
Preserved Fruit - Aix-en-Provence, France

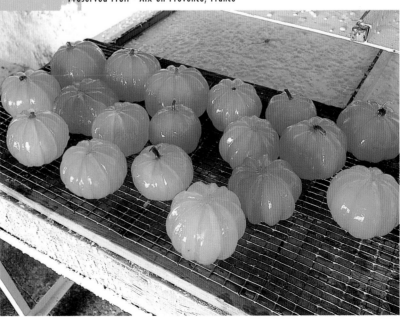

Technical Details
6x4.5cm Single Lens Reflex - 55-
110mm zoom lens, extension tube,
1/2 sec at f22, Fuji Provia.

A Holiday Diary

It has to be admitted that even the most enthusiastic of photographers can be tempted into the "I'll do it later" philosophy when on a relaxing vacation and having a hard-earned rest. I know I am sometimes. If you succumb, this is often followed, two days before the return flight, by simply whizzing round with a hand-held camera and shooting a few "stand and smile" snaps out of sheer guilt. One way to overcome this temptation is to motivate yourself with a project, such as keeping a visual holiday diary. It is well worthwhile making a wish list of pictures you would like to have and, if you're really keen, it could begin with preparations such as looking at maps and guide books, packing the suitcase or loading the car.

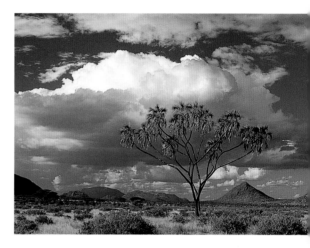

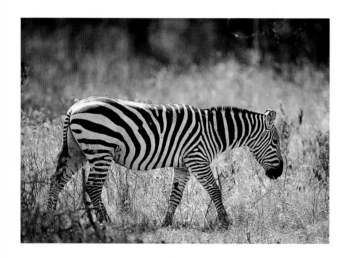

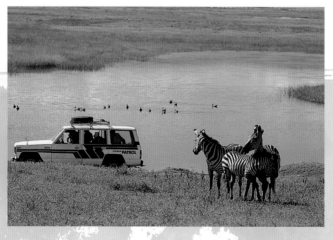

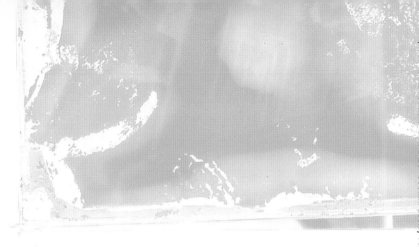

Technical Details
35mm SLR Camera with a 20–600mm zoom, Fuji Provia and Velvia.

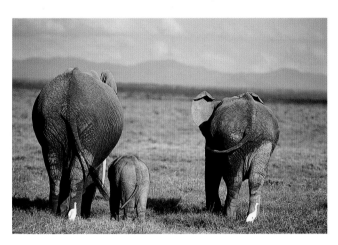

The photographs on the following three pages were all taken during a holiday in Africa when I made a conscious attempt to capture something of all the experiences the trip provided. I'm not a great devotee of the "stand and smile" approach but there are occasions when this type of shot is needed. The danger is when these pictures begin to dominate a collection.

Rule of Thumb

When taking your diary pictures try to vary the style and quality of the images. Make sure you have close-ups as well as longer shots, find ways of varying both the lighting and colour quality of your pictures, use different focal lengths to obtain a variety of perspective effects and photograph views and architecture as well as people. This will help to make your holiday diary interesting to all who see it.

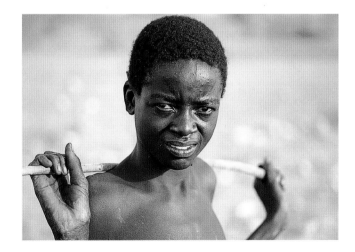

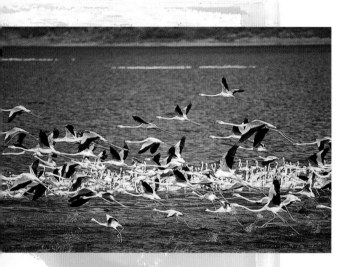

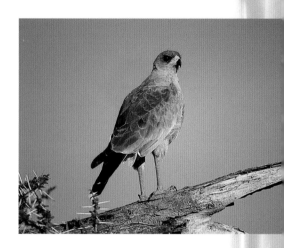

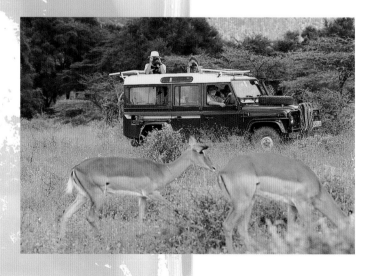

Technical Details
35mm SLR Camera with a 20–600mm zoom lens, Fuji Provia and Velvia.

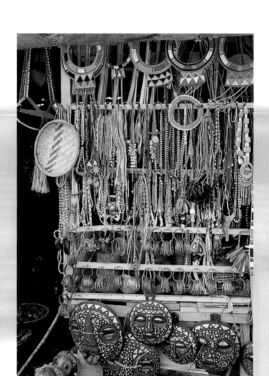

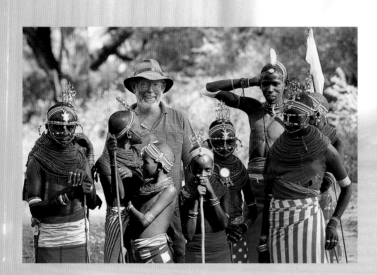

A Holiday Diary

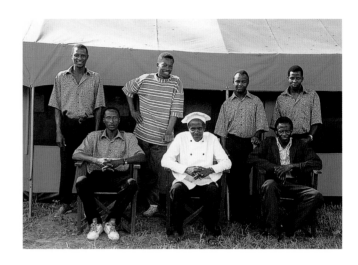

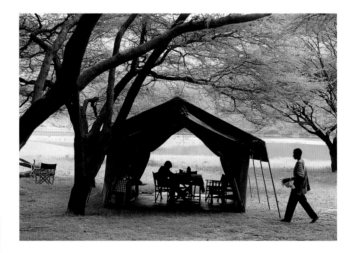

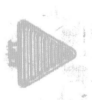

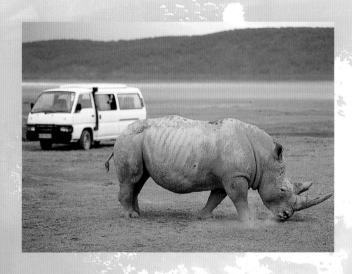

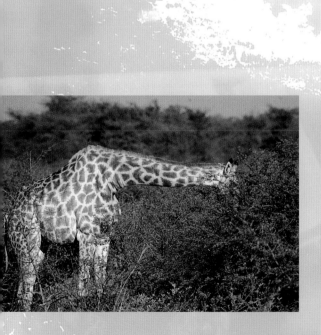

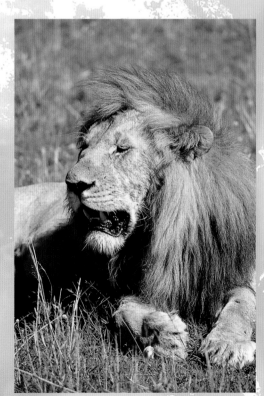

Technical Details
35mm SLR Camera with a 20–600mm zoom lens, Fuji Provia and Velvia.

Shooting a Photo Essay

The majority of photographs are taken with the intention of standing alone, to be viewed as single, independant images. But this can be a rather limiting way of regarding photography and often the desire to include as much information as possible during that single decisive moment, when the exposure is made, is the biggest factor in producing photographs which have little visual appeal and impact.

While some images are powerful enough to stand alone, hung on a gallery wall, for example, or used as a magazine cover or double-page spread, they often do not tell the viewer as much about the place or subject as a sequence of images can in the form of a photo essay.

The key to shooting a photo story is the ability to think in terms of how the images you are producing will look when viewed as a collection, as they might be laid out on a double-page spread of a magazine, for instance. The main thing is to consider how each picture affects the ones adjacent to it and vice versa.

location
The Wine Harvest - France

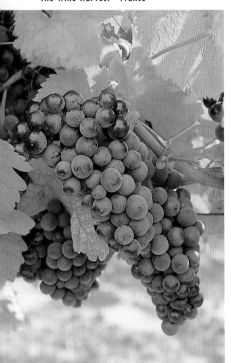

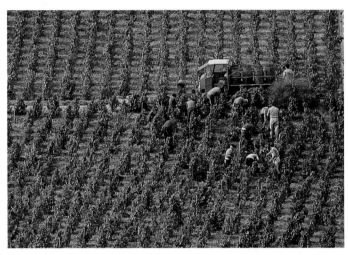

Technique

There are essentially two ways of shooting a photo essay, one is to produce a chronological coverage of an event in a recognisable sequence and the other is to build up a composite image of a place by photographing a series of isolated aspects of a location and linking them together.

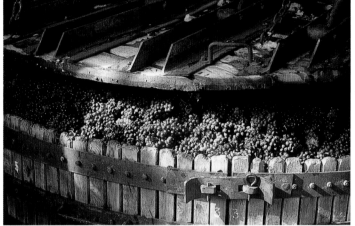

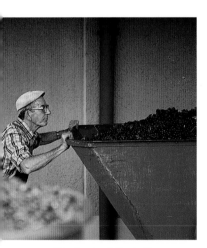

Technique

It also helps to vary the **colour** quality and content of your shots so that some images are bold and fully **saturated** and others have a softer and more pastel quality. You can also vary the subject matter of your photographs so that a shot of a building is seen in **sequence** with say a portrait or a landscape.

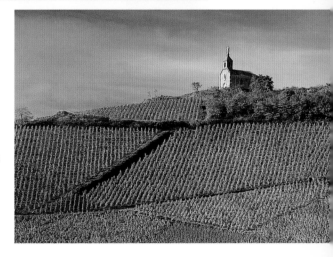

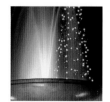

Composition & Light

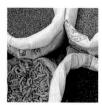

3

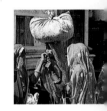

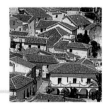

It's vital to devote time to the
technical aspects of taking pictures —
finding the right viewpoint, composing the subject well and waiting until the light is at its most
evocative. Sometimes it's not the most obvious approaches which produce the best pictures —
as you will see in this chapter.

Choosing a Viewpoint

Many people will take a photograph from the place where they first see a subject. The camera's viewpoint is, however, one of the most important factors in determining the success of a photograph and should be the result of careful consideration. It can be surprising how much difference just a metre, or even less, can make to the composition of an image and it is always worth exploring all of the possibilities before making your exposure.

Seeing

The pretty seaside village of Collioure in France is one of the most photogenic spots on the Mediterranean coast – it's a favourite of mine and of countless others. Once part of a thriving anchovy fleet the few freshly-painted boats which are pulled up on the small beach are now there, I suspect, for the benefit of photographers.

Thinking

My visit on this occasion was on a spring afternoon and the sun was in a position which made this view of the old harbour-side church quite pleasing as well as lighting the boat very nicely. The only problem was there were a few people sitting on the beach which made the scene look very untidy.

Technical Details
▼ Medium-format SLR Camera with a 50mm wide-angle lens, 81C warm-up and polarising filters, and Fuji Velvia.

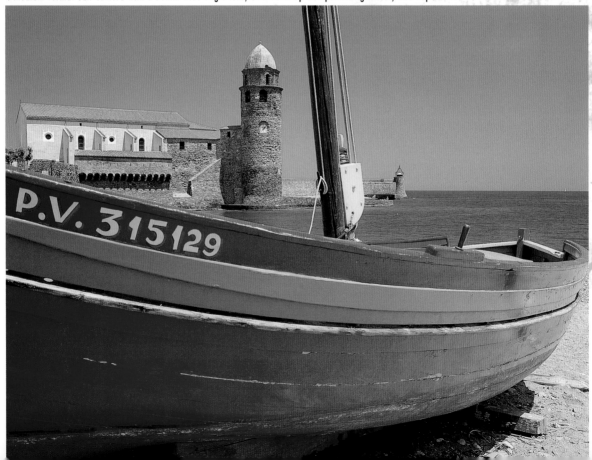

▲Technical Details
Medium-format SLR Camera with a 50mm wide-angle lens, 81C warm-up and polarising filters, and Fuji Velvia.

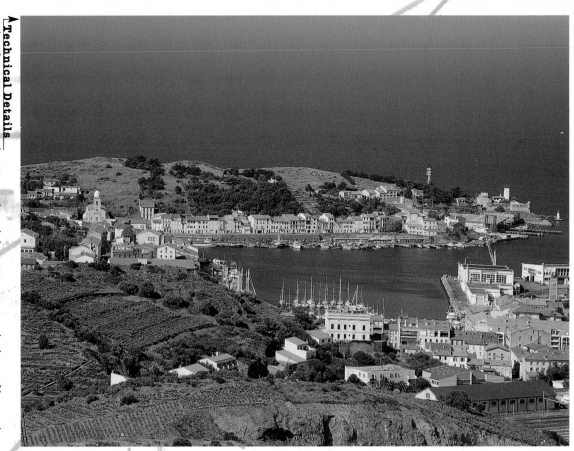

This photograph was taken on the same day a little further down the coast above the village of Port Vendres. I chose a viewpoint which placed some vineyards in the foreground to add an element of contrast and increase the impression of depth and distance, and used a polarising filter to increase the colour saturation and the clarity of the scene.

Acting

I had intended to use the boat as **foreground interest** in any case but, on setting up my camera, I **became aware** that by moving half a metre or so lower than I originally planned and a little closer to it I could **hide** the unwanted human interest quite easily behind it. I used a **wide-angle** lens to include enough of the boat in the frame and set a **small aperture** to ensure there was enough depth of field.

Rule of Thumb

Most photographs are taken at eye level from a standing position, because this is what is most comfortable. But often a slightly lower or higher viewpoint can make a considerable difference, especially when there are objects close to the camera and when a wide-angle lens is being used.

Choosing a Viewpoint

Seeing

I was travelling through the hill country in Sri Lanka in a region where tea is widely grown. The patterns created by the rows of terraced bushes were the thing which first struck me and so too did the rich green colour of the landscape.

Thinking

My first thought was to look for a feature within the plantation such as a hut or some tea pickers which could act as a focus of attention within the image but there was nothing which seemed interesting enough. I then became aware of the striking contrast which the red-soil pathways created in between the bushes.

Technical Details

35mm SLR Camera with a 35–70mm zoom lens, 81B warm-up and polarising filters, and Fuji Velvia.

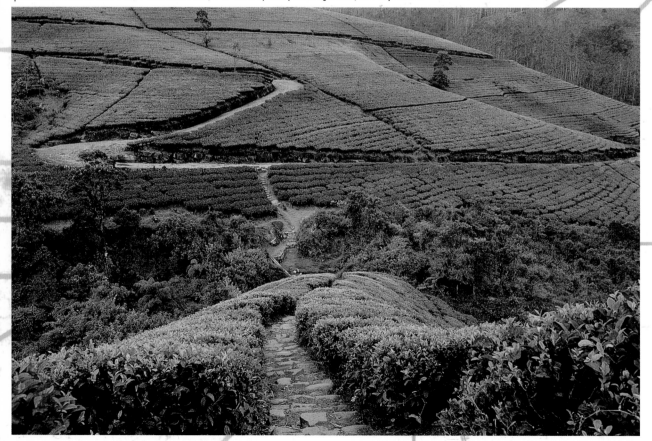

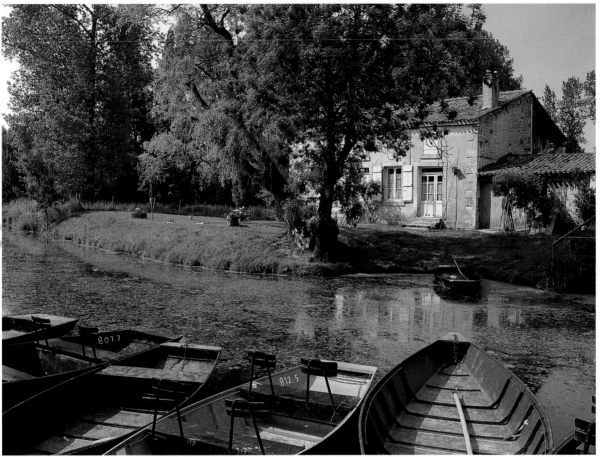

Technical Details
Medium-format SLR Camera with a 50mm wide-angle lens, 81C warm-up and polarising filters, and Fuji Velvia.

My choice of viewpoint for this shot, taken in the Marais Poitevin region of south-west France, was largely determined by my wish to include these boats in the foreground. This has added both to the atmosphere and interest of the picture as well as enhancing its three-dimensional quality. I used a small aperture to ensure that the details in both the nearest and furthest parts of the scene were recorded in sharp focus.

Acting

I found a viewpoint which made one of the paths come directly towards the camera and, at the same time, showed it zig-zagging away into the corner of the frame. It was overcast and raining at the time and I framed the image to exclude the pale sky which would have detracted from the strong effect of the green foliage.

Rule of Thumb

The effect of perspective in a scene is the result of both the choice of viewpoint and of the focal length of the lens being used. When a wide-angle lens is used with objects close to the camera as well as far away the perspective will be exaggerated, increasing the impression of depth and distance. Contrarily, when a long-focus lens is used from a more distant viewpoint the effect of perspective will be diminished, producing an image with a more two-dimensional quality.

Choosing a Viewpoint

Seeing

One of the numerous small beaches on the Caribbean island of Tobago was the location for this shot. The scene appealed to me because the sunlight was crisp and there was a good blue sky with some beautiful white clouds.

Thinking

The angle of the sunlight meant, however, that the scene was lit much more pleasingly when viewed in this direction and this narrowed down my choice of viewpoint considerably. I also wanted to have some foreground interest as, no matter how stunning it is, an empty, featureless beach seldom makes a satisfying photograph.

Technical Details
▼ 35mm SLR Camera with a 24–85mm zoom lens, 81C warm-up and polarising filters, and Fuji Velvia.

A journey through South Australia's outback country led to this shot. I wanted to capture something of the remoteness of the countryside and the emptiness of the roads. Although you could be forgiven for thinking that not much changed in many miles of driving I chose this particular viewpoint for a number of reasons. Firstly, I liked the fact that the distant curve in the road made it seem to disappear. Secondly, from here the mountain range was ideally placed in relation to the direction of the road, and finally the cloud formation seemed particularly impressive at this point. I framed the shot so that the horizon was placed along the lower third of the frame in order to make the most of the sky.

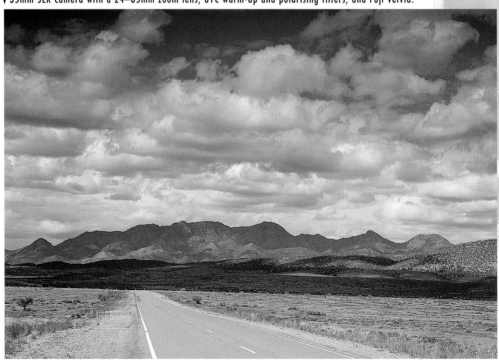

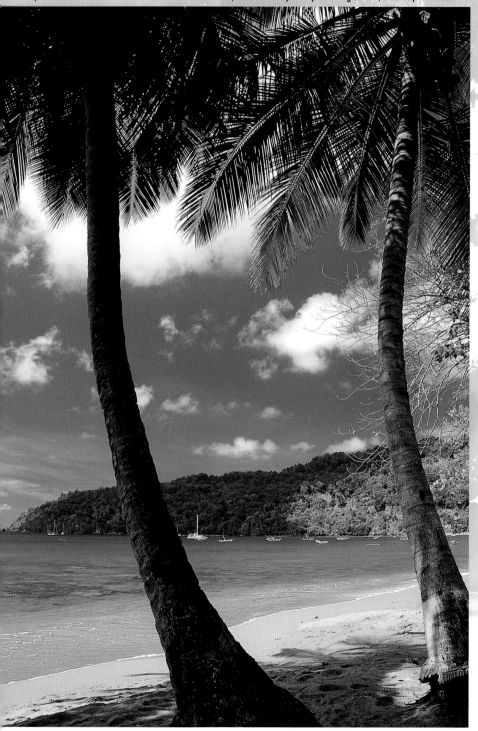

Acting

These two partially silhouetted palm trees at the edge of the beach were ideal and I opted to use the upright format in order to emphasise their elegant curving trunks and to include the clouds at the top of the frame. I made a final, fine adjustment to the viewpoint to reveal the small white boat in the distance and also to hide a rather ugly shack on the hillside behind the left-hand palm tree.

Rule of Thumb

There is an easy way of remembering how a change of viewpoint will affect the objects on different planes within an image. If you move to the right, objects close to the camera will appear to move to the left in relation to distant details, and vice versa. If you move further from your subject it will appear to become smaller in relation to more distant objects – and vice versa – but they will also be shown closer to their true relative sizes.

Choosing a Viewpoint

Seeing

Watching this giant paella being made is like seeing a piece of theatre, the pan is well over a metre in diameter and it feeds more than 50 people. The initial reaction is to capture the action of the cook as he tips in bucketfuls of ingredients and stirs them with a huge paddle.

Thinking

But I also wanted to show the sizzling, colourful nature of the dish cooking as well as the process of making it and decided to use a very close viewpoint to show the colour and texture of the food to its best advantage.

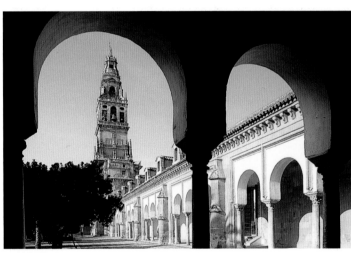

Acting

I used a wide-angle lens because this allowed me to shoot from very close to the pan and slightly above it while still being able to include all of the dish in the frame, together with the wood-fire flames flicking around its edges.

location
The Cathedral courtyard, Cordoba - Andalucia, Spain

Rule of Thumb

When considering your choice of viewpoint it pays to look behind you as well as at your subject because it's often possible to find foreground details which can act as a frame to the composition, as in this picture taken through the arches of the Cathedral close. This can add an element of impact to the image as well as increasing the impression of depth.

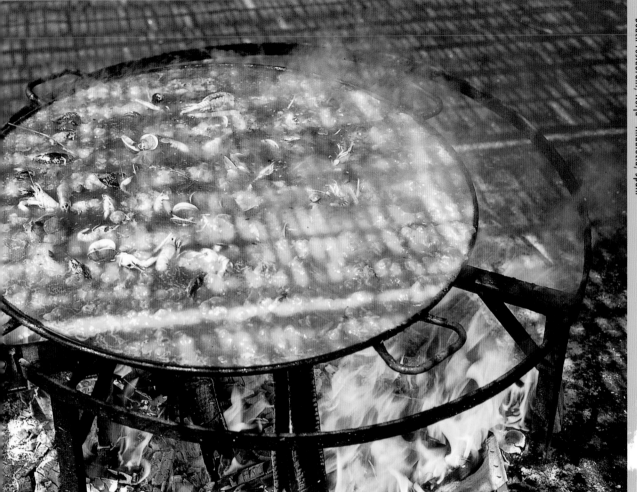

Technical Details
35mm Single Lens Reflex - 28mm perspective control lens,
polarising and 81C warm-up filters, Fuji Velvia.

Technical Details
35mm Rangefinder Camera - 28mm lens,
Kodak Ektachrome E100SW.

Using Shapes & Patterns

Photographs depend for their effect on a number of individual visual elements and the most successful photographs are usually those in which one or more of these elements is boldly and clearly defined. The outline or shape of a subject is the element which usually first identifies it and a photograph with a boldly-defined shape invariably has a strong impact. Subjects which contain a simple, basic shape like a circle or triangle are often among those which create the most eye-catching images.

Seeing

The very dominant colour and interesting shapes of these shuttered windows caught my eye while travelling through a French village. Even the creeper had a strong shape and colour and the neutral background made a good contrast for both.

Thinking

I wanted to frame the image as tightly as possible, to emphasise the shapes and colour and also to exclude adjacent details which would have spoiled the balance of the image.

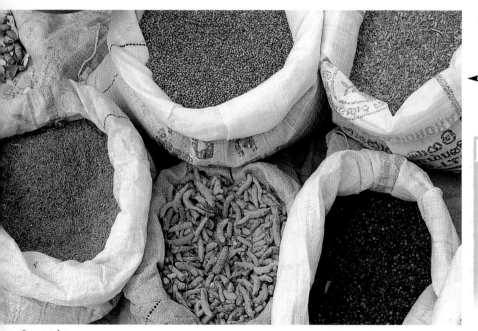

Technical Details
35mm Single Lens Reflex - 150mm lens, 81B warm-up filter, Fuji Velvia.

Technical Details
35mm Single Lens Reflex - 50mm lens, Kodak Ektachrome 64.

Rule of Thumb

When shooting on colour print film it's not worth using warm-up filters. The effect of a polarising filter will be beneficial with both types of film.
There are two types of polarising filter - Linear and Circular - and the former can cause interference with some auto-focus and exposure-control systems. If in doubt, buy a circular polariser.

location
Street Market - Marrakesh, Morocco

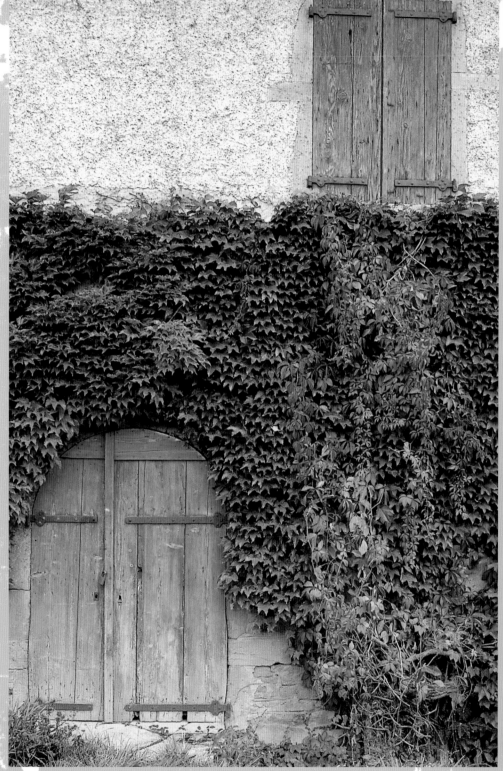

Acting

I used a **long-focus** lens to isolate the **section** of the house which made the most effective composition and framed the image so that a shutter appeared in each corner, creating a **diagonal** line. I used a tripod to avoid the risk of camera shake and to help me **frame** the image very precisely.

location
A village house near Beaujeu - Rhone, France

Using Shapes & Patterns

Rule of Thumb

The impression of a pattern is created when a distinctive shape is repeated within the image and it can have a powerful impact when used as part of a composition. The effect of a pattern is most telling when there is an element within the image which creates a contrast with it, such as the Cafe lettering among the shapes created by these shuttered windows.

Seeing

The shapes of the trees and the pattern created by the rows of vines had, I felt, the potential for a strong image. The effect was helped considerably by the fact that the trees were silhouetted against a lighter-toned background and the vines formed lines running directly towards them.

Thinking

The most telling part of the scene was actually quite a small area of the overall view and I thought the photograph would have more impact if I excluded the sky, which was quite pale and hazy.

Acting

Because of this I decided to use a very long-focus lens to isolate the most effective part of the scene. I fitted a polarising filter to increase the colour saturation of the foliage and a warm-up filter to further enhance the green of the vines.

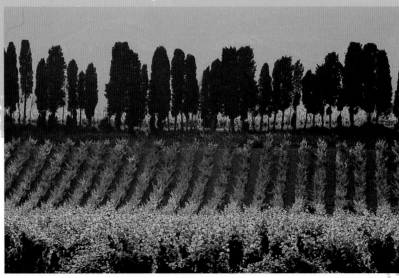

location
Vineyards near Carcassonne - Languedoc Roussillon, France

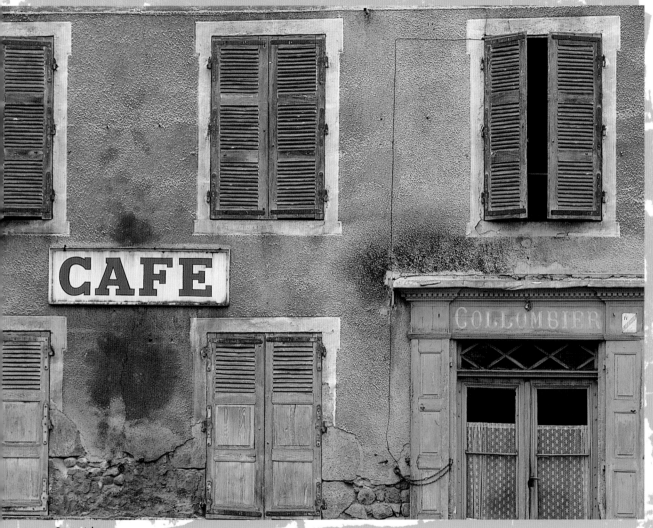

Technical Details
35mm Single Lens Reflex -
80-200mm zoom lens, Fuji Velvia.

CAFE

COLLOMBIER

location
Mauriac - Auvergne, France

Technical Details
35mm Single Lens Reflex - 300mm lens,
polarising and 81C warm-up filters,
Fuji Velvia.

Technique

When shooting subjects like this on a long-focus lens it is vital to use a tripod and cable release to obtain maximum image sharpness and it is also preferable to lock the camera's mirror up a few seconds before making the exposure so that the vibration caused as it flips up will not affect the image sharpness.

Form & Texture

The element of form gives the image a feeling of solidity and is dependent upon the direction and quality of light. A soft directional light will create a gradual transition of tone within the subject from highlight to shadow whereas a hard light will produce a more abrupt graduation from light to dark.

Seeing

It was the rich texture of this old stone wall which first caught my eye emphasised by the strong sunlight glancing along its surface from the side. But I also liked the contrasting V shape of the roof with the circular wheel.

Thinking

I felt that the most striking effect would be created by shooting the wall front on and framing the image so the roof was at the top of the frame and the base of the wheel at the bottom.

Acting

I also wanted to reduce the effect of perspective making the wall appear as flat as possible to the camera so I used a fairly distant viewpoint and fitted a long-focus zoom lens to frame the image precisely.

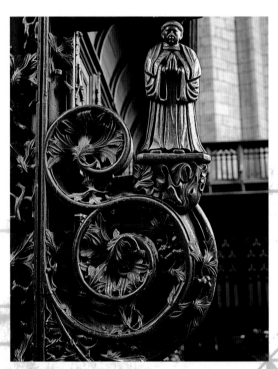

location
The Cathedral of Villefranche de Rouergue - Midi Pyrenees, France

In this shot of a medieval carving the quite soft light from a window is directed fairly acutely from one side of the subject and created a full range of tones from highlight to shadow making it look solid and three-dimensional.

Texture is an element which is, in effect, the form within a surface, like a weathered stone wall, for instance and can be used to create images with rich tones and a strong tactile sense. As a general rule, the effect of texture is strongest when the light is directed from a fairly acute angle to the surface.

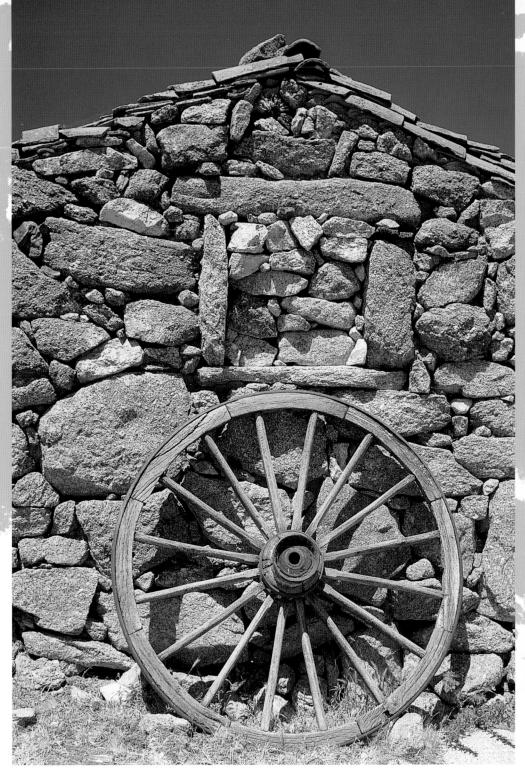

location
An ancient farm near Avila - Castile Leon, Spain

Exploiting Perspective

Perspective is the effect created by the diminishing size of objects as they recede from the camera, such as looking down a tree-lined avenue, for instance. It's a valuable way of helping to give an image a sense of depth and distance and also contributes to the impression of solidity and the three-dimensional quality which a photograph can have.

Seeing

It was the quality of evening light on this seascape which attracted me with the effect which it had on the colours and textures of the old weathered groyne supports and the shingle.

Thinking

I considered a number of options concerning the viewpoint but finally thought that shooting along the row of posts and exaggerating the perspective might add interest to the seascape as well as creating a more dynamic composition.

Rule of Thumb

The effect of perspective varies according to the relative distances between the camera, the nearest objects and those furthest away. If the image includes both foreground objects along with distant ones the perspective effect will be marked. so that, for instance, a person can appear much larger than a distant building. But if there is no immediate foreground and all the principle objects are some distance away from the camera there will be a minimal suggestion of perspective and objects will be shown close to their true relative size.

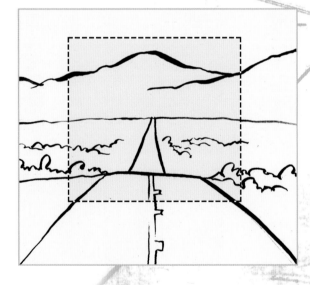

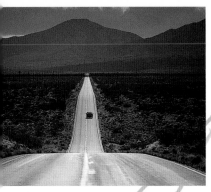

location
Death Valley - California, USA

Technical Details
35mm Single Lens Reflex -
300mm lens, 81C warm-up and
neutral-graduated filters,
Kodak Ektachrome 64.

Technical Details
35mm Single Lens Reflex -
20mm lens, neutral-graduated filter,
1/4 sec 2 f22, Fuji Velvia.

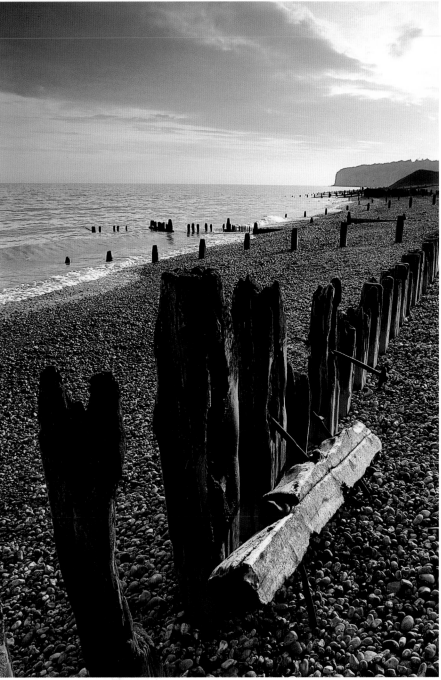

Acting

I chose a viewpoint a little to the
land ward side of the posts so that
I could see along the row and
also across them to the sea. I
fitted my widest angle lens
and moved the camera as
close as I could to the nearest
post in order to accentuate the perspective as much as
possible. I set the smallest possible aperture to ensure the image
was sharp from the nearest to the furthest detail and I fitted a
neutral graduated filter to make the sky a little darker.

location
Winchelsea Beach - East Sussex, UK

Exploiting Perspective

Seeing

Looking down from a high viewpoint revealed the pattern created by the rooftops of these village houses and this was the element of the scene which most appealed to me.

Thinking

I considered including some of the hillside and sky on the far side of the village but ultimately decided that the most striking effect would be to frame the image tightly with a long focus lens and minimise the perspective effect making the image seem to be on one plane.

Acting

I chose a viewpoint very close to the edge of the hill which enabled me to shoot directly down to exclude the foreground and framed the image so the shapes of the rooftops and white house fronts created the most pleasing arrangement.

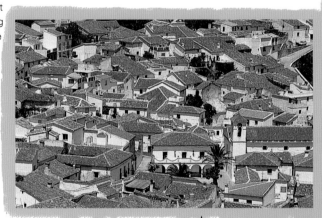

location
Algatocin - Andalucia, Spain

Technical Details
6x4.5cm Single Lens Reflex -
200mm lens, 81C warm-up
filter, Fuji Velvia.

Technical Details
35mm Single Lens Reflex -
20mm lens, polarising and 81C
warm-up filters, Fuji Velvia.

Rule of Thumb

The use of a wide-angle lens when close foreground details are included in the frame helps to make pictures taken from both high and low viewpoints more dramatic, as in this shot of fishermen photographed from close to ground level.

location
Mombasa - Kenya

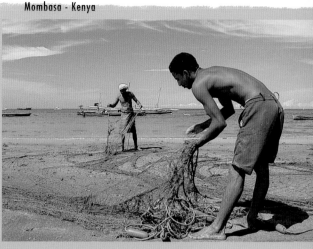

Technical Details ➤
35mm Single Lens Reflex - 24mm lens, polarising and 81C warm-up filters, Fuji Velvia.

location
A farm near Tours - Loire, France

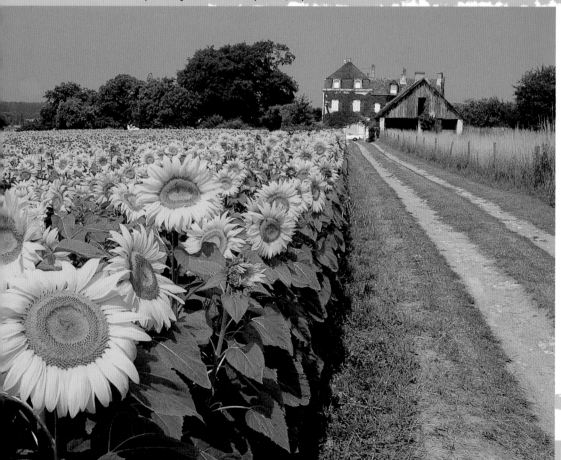

For this picture I chose a viewpoint which used the perspective effect to create bold diagonal lines which converged towards the farmhouse and emphasised its role as the main point of interest and also accentuated the impression of depth and distance in the image.

Composing the Image

Having decided on a viewpoint the next step is to decide just how much of a scene should be included in the frame and how much should be left out. It may well be that this decision may lead to the need to make a change in the viewpoint but it is being aware of this relationship between viewpoint and the way the image is framed which is the key to creating an eye-catching composition.

Seeing

The island of Burano in Italy's Veneto region is an extremely colourful place where every house seems to be painted a different, and very bright, colour. This row of houses alongside a small canal is one of the most photogenic corners and I arrived just as the sun had moved high enough in the sky to begin glancing along the front of the houses.

Thinking

I began with the thought of adopting a more frontal angle on the houses but this meant a more distant viewpoint which included too many obtrusive details on the canal side. On taking up a viewpoint much closer to the edge of the quayside and looking along the row of houses at a more acute angle, I found the diagonal line this created gave the composition more life.

Acting

From this viewpoint, however, I needed to use a wide-angle lens and this created too much empty space on the left-hand side of the frame. It was then that I considered using the panoramic format which has cropped the image more tightly at the top and bottom of the frame, making the image more compact and eliminating the excessive amount of sky and quayside on the left of the picture.

Technical Details
▼35mm Viewfinder Camera with a 45mm wide-angle lens, 81B warm-up and polarising filters, and Fuji Velvia.

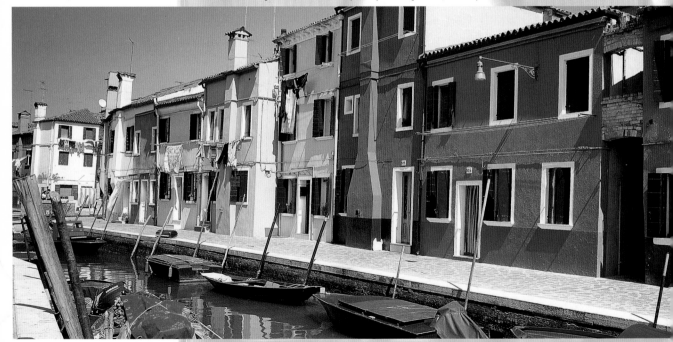

Medium-format SLR Camera with a 50mm wide-angle lens, 81B warm-up and polarising filters, and Fuji Velvia.

I saw this tranquil scene in the region called La Grande Briere in western France, a web of lakes and reed-lined creeks with a rather mystical atmosphere. I arrived there early one morning to find the water absolutely motionless and the sun had just climbed high enough to begin illuminating this collection of moored boats. I chose my viewpoint to look along the row towards the single, brightly painted vessel which has created a focus of attention. I used a wide-angle lens and set a small aperture to ensure there was enough depth of field.

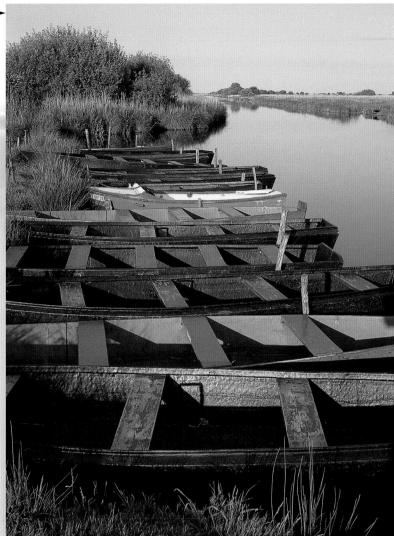

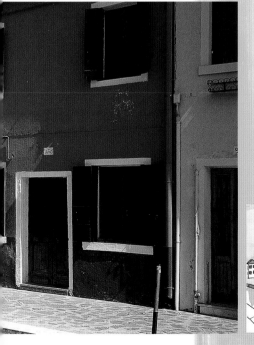

Rule of Thumb

There is seldom just one best way of composing an image and an inherently photogenic scene can invariably be framed in a variety of ways. You can learn a great deal about composition by shooting a few variations and then comparing the results; you may well find that the shot you thought would be the most successful is sometimes bettered by another.

Composing the Image

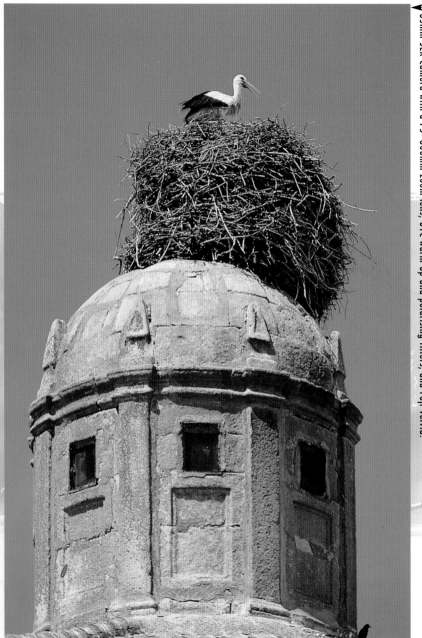

Technical Details
35mm SLR Camera with a 75–300mm zoom lens, 81C warm-up and polarising filters, and Fuji Velvia.

Storks' nests are a common sight in Spain during the summer; at times it seems that almost every church tower has one. This shot was taken near Avila in the village of Piedrahita. I was lucky to to find such a good nest perched upon such an attractive tower and lit so nicely, and I only had to wait a short while before the stork appeared. I simply used a long-focus lens to frame the image as tightly as possible, including just enough sky around the subject for comfort.

Rule of Thumb

It is very easy when using the viewfinder to concentrate so much on aiming the camera accurately at the main subject that you are not fully aware of all the other details which are being included. This often results in the subject seeming smaller in the picture than you originally thought. It's a good habit to always check around the edges of the frame before shooting.

Seeing

An antique store Moroccan-style, I came across this extraordinary **emporium** near the town of Zagora in southern Morocco and was charmed by both the store and its **proprietor**, (who was a world-class salesman).

Thinking

He **readily agreed** to stand in the doorway while I photographed the shop front, I placed him there because the **dark interior** made his white robe **stand out** very clearly.

Acting

I decided to **frame the image** so that he appeared in the right-hand quarter of the frame and the **pot** perched on the roof occupied the very **top left-hand** corner. I felt that these two elements **balanced** each other quite nicely.

Technical Details

35mm SLR Camera with a 20–35mm zoom lens, 81C warm-up and polarising filters, and Fuji Velvia.

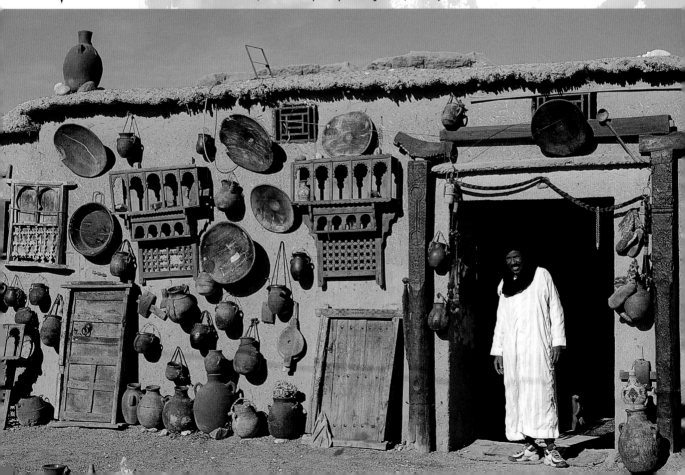

Composing the Image

Seeing

This pretty painted cottage is in the village of Gerberoy in the Picardy region of France, a place **famous for its roses**, and where a rose festival is held each June. My attention was caught by the **striking contrast** between the bright **blue timbers** of the cottage and the rich red of the rose bush.

Thinking

It was a heavily **overcast day** and had been raining but the soft light enhanced the **rich colours** of the subject. However, the sky was white and I looked for ways in which I could exclude it but still show a **large area** of the scene. My first thought was to shoot from quite square-on to the right-hand wall of the cottage and **frame the image tightly**. This worked quite well but I felt that not enough of the scene was being seen to show the charm of the small house.

Acting

By fitting a wide-angle lens and taking up a **viewpoint** quite close to the corner of the building, I found I was able to include a much larger area of it and still **crop out** the sky. This more interesting angle with its **diagonal lines** also gave the composition a rather more dynamic quality.

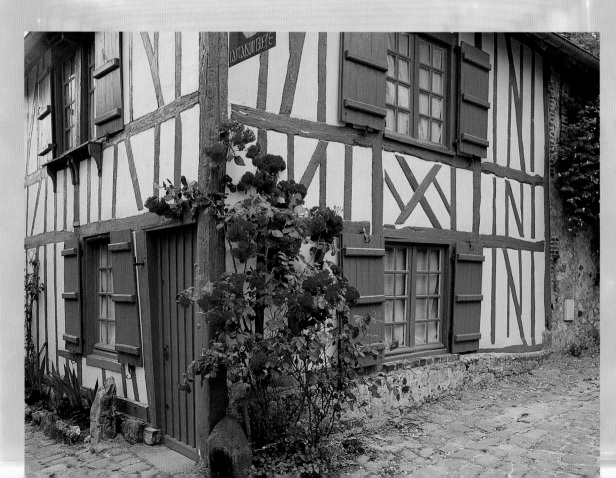

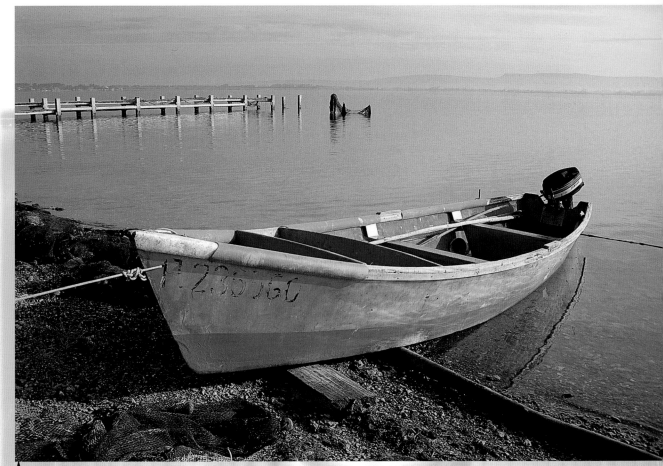

↑**Technical Details**
  35mm SLR Camera with a 20—35mm zoom lens, 81B warm-up and polarising filters, and Fuji Velvia.

For this picture, taken beside the Etang de Bages in the Languedoc region of France, I was attracted by the calm, mirror-like surface of the water and the overall blueness of the image which was relieved only by the splashes of red on the boat. I used a wide-angle lens from a viewpoint close to the boat and framed the image to show as wide an area of the lake as possible.

Rule of Thumb

The golden rule of composition states that the strongest place for the centre of interest in an image is where lines dividing the picture area into thirds horizontally and vertically meet. This will nearly always produce a pleasing effect but should not be followed slavishly. It's best to learn how to identify all of the key elements in an image and to frame a scene in such a way that an overall balance is created between them.

◄**Technical Details**
  Medium-format SLR Camera with a 50mm wide-angle lens, an 81A warm-up filter, and Fuji Velvia.

Composing the Image

Seeing

The blaze of red from this poppy field was visible from some distance away and it took me only a short time to find the field. It was not only the colours of the poppies which appealed to me but also the row of trees and distant hillside.

Thinking

I walked along the edge of the field from which I could look across to the hill beyond, and which also placed the sun to one side producing a pleasing lighting quality. I eventually found a viewpoint which placed a good area of the poppies in an effective juxtaposition with the trees and a attractive section of the distant hillside.

Acting

It occurred to me that there were three distinct bands of colour, the pale blue sky, the strong green of the trees and hillside and the red poppies in the foreground. I decided to make this the crux of the composition choosing an upright format and using my zoom lens to adjust the framing so the three bands of colour were almost equal in area. I used a polarising filter to add strength to the colour of the sky and increase the colour saturation of the poppies.

Technical Details
6x4.5cm Single Lens Reflex - 55-110 zoom lens, polarising and 81C warm-up filters, Fuji Velvia.

Technical Details
35mm Single Lens Reflex - 50mm lens, Kodak Ektachrome 64.

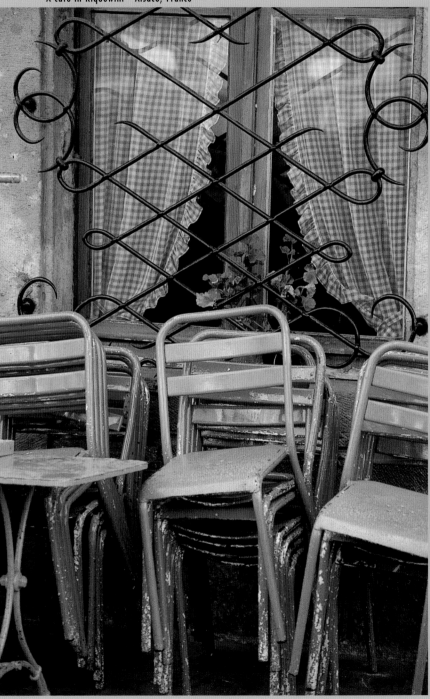

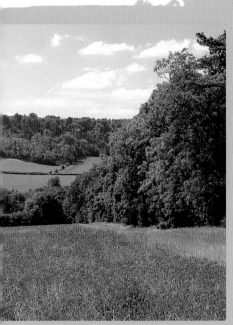

The contrasting colours of the blue chairs and the net curtain combined with the shapes they created suggested to me that I should frame this shot so that they were almost equal in area. I included a little of the wall and refrained from using a fully frontal viewpoint to prevent the composition becoming too symmetrical.

Design by Colour

One of the most effective ways of producing striking, eye-catching images is by the careful use of colour. Inexperienced photographers often fall into the trap of believing that very colourful subjects make the best colour photographs. The opposite is closer to the truth, the more restricted the use of colour the more telling the result.

Technical Details
35mm Single Lens Reflex - 80-200mm zoom lens, 81C warm-up and neutral-graduated filters, Fuji Velvia.

location
Chateau Latour and its Vineyard, Pauillac - Gironde, France

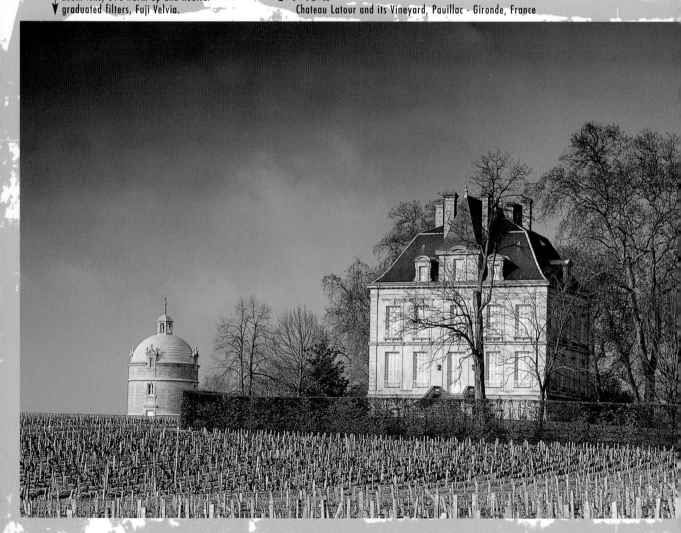

Seeing

This chateau and its distinctive tower is a well-known feature of the Medoc vineyards and I wanted to find a way of showing them both together. It was a winter morning, quite early, and the lighting from the more obvious viewpoint, showing the front of the chateau with the tower in the foreground, was unattractive.

Thinking

I decided to take a slow drive round the chateau, through its vineyards, heading in a direction which I thought would produce a more pleasing lighting effect. To my surprise I found that as I passed along this side of the chateau I could still see the tower and the sunlight was glancing off the stone in a very striking way.

Acting

As I was now a fair distance from the building I decided to use a long-focus lens to crop out some of the vineyard in the foreground and to give me a good-sized image of the chateau and tower. The lighting had already made the grey wintry sky seem quite dark but I used a neutral-graduated filter to increase this effect and an 81C warm-up filter to add some richness to the colour of the stone.

location
A street scene in Jaipur - Rajasthan, India

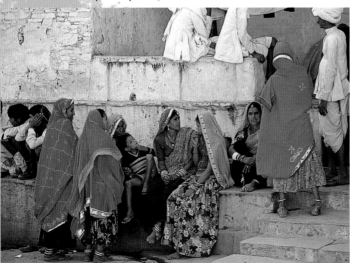

Rule of Thumb

As a general rule, brightly coloured subjects, such as this street scene, for instance, will photograph more pleasingly with a soft light, like that of a cloudy or hazy day, or in this case in open shade.

◄ Technical Details
35mm Single Lens Reflex -
35-70mm zoom lens, Fuji Provia.

Design by Colour

Seeing

I was travelling in the late autumn through the countryside near Chambery in the French Alps when I came across this stunning tree with the most vivid red leaves. The sky was slightly hazy and consequently the sunlight was not quite as sharp and clear as I would have liked.

Thinking

I decided that it would be most striking if I could find a viewpoint where it would be contrasted against the reasonably blue sky or the green foliage surrounding it.

This attractive waterfall is near the village of Baumes les Messieurs in the Jura region of France. I took this picture in the spring when the foliage was very fresh and light in colour. It was this colour which appealed to me about the scene and I framed the image so that green became the dominant colour of the image. I used a small aperture to enable the use of a slow shutter speed which has recorded the moving water as a soft, smoke-like blur.

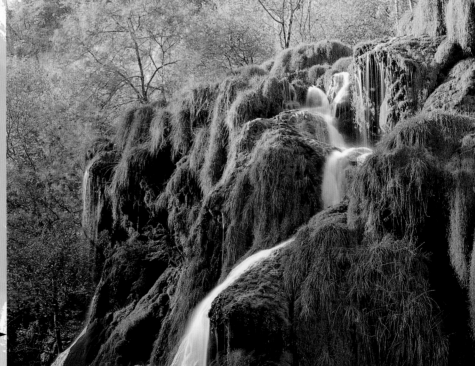

Technical Details
Medium-format SLR Camera with a 150mm lens, 81C warm-up and polarising filters, and Fuji Velvia.

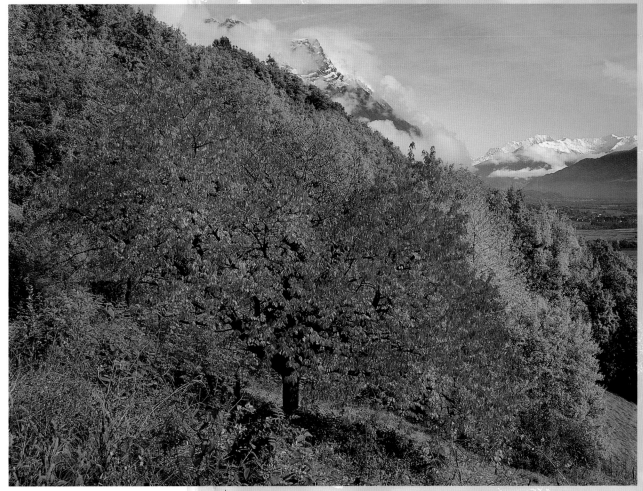

▲Technical Details

Medium-format SLR Camera with a 50mm wide-angle lens, 81C warm-up, neutral-graduated and polarising filters, and Fuji Velvia.

Acting

I finally found this spot where a slightly lower viewpoint placed the tree against the bluest part of the sky, and also allowed me to frame it in such a way that it was also bordered by green. I liked the way the tree created a diagonal red band across the frame. I used a polarising filter to increase the colour saturation, a neutral-graduated filter to make the blue sky as dark as possible and a warm-up filter to further enhance the red.

Rule of Thumb

Colour contrast is one of the most effective ways of creating impact in a colour photograph, especially when the image is restricted to two dominant colours which are far apart in the spectrum — for example, blue contrasted with yellow or red with blue. The effect can be quite striking when a small area of one colour is set against a background of the opposite hue.

Design by Colour

Seeing

Although blue is a commonplace colour in nature, I always find it very interesting in other situations and when I spotted these blue rain covers on the moored gondolas during a trip to Venice, I felt there was the possibility of an interesting picture.

Thinking

The background of the lagoon water also had a bluish quality but at the same time showed up the elegant shapes of the crafts very effectively. I also like the poles which created a contrasting shape and a patterned effect within the scene.

Technical Details

35mm SLR Camera with a 100–300mm zoom lens and Fuji Velvia.

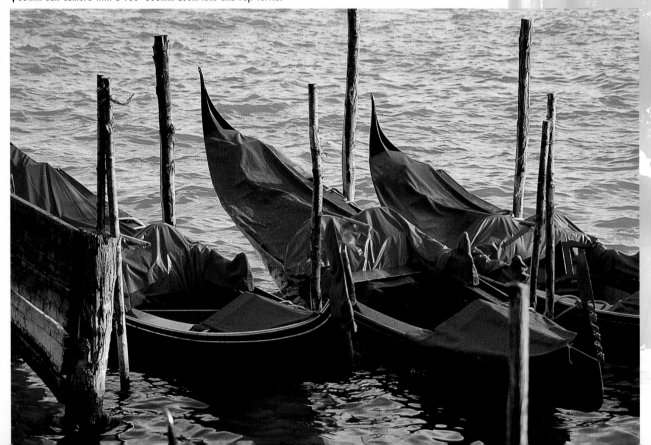

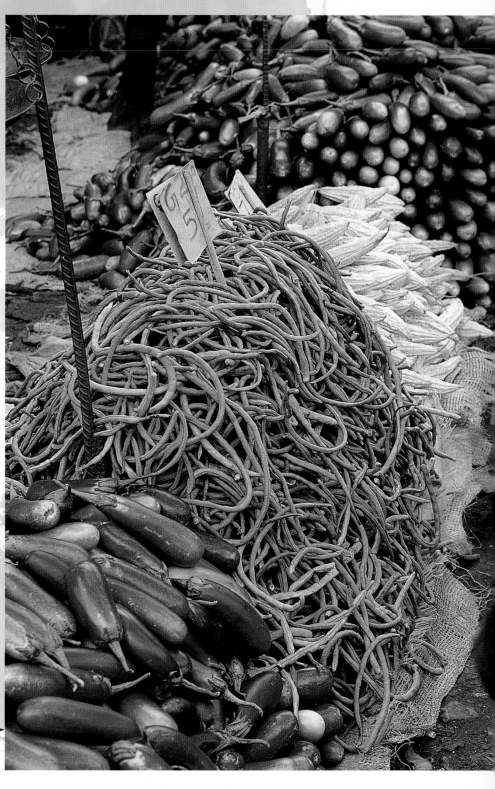

Acting

There was a large number of gondolas tied up at this spot and it was necessary to find a **viewpoint** from which I could separate just a few from the crowd. From this spot I was able to **frame just three** crafts at the end of the group, using a **long-focus lens**, in a way which emphasised their shape and which also gave me a pleasingly balanced **arrangement** of poles.

I spotted this display of vegetables while wandering around a country market in Sri Lanka and was struck by the juxtaposition of green and purple. I found a viewpoint which allowed me to include some of the aubergines in the foreground and framed the shot to include the other pile in the background.

Technical Details
35mm SLR Camera with a 35–70mm zoom lens, an 81A warm-up filter and Fuji Provia.

Magic of Light

Modern films, cameras and accessories make it possible to take photographs when there is little or no light, but just because it's possible does not mean that the outcome will necessarily be pleasing. The quality and direction of light is vital to the success of a photograph and while good lighting can bring a picture to life, so too can a poorly lit scene produce a disappointing result, even when the image is interesting and well composed.

Seeing

I took this photograph on the Brittany coast of France near Morlaix one summer evening. I could see earlier on in the afternoon that there was the likelihood of an interesting sunset and, while travelling around, had been looking for a possible viewpoint. Water and sunsets can be a powerful combination but some other interest is usually necessary to produce a satisfying photograph.

Thinking

I'd made a note of this small beach with the boats and promontory and when the sun began to go down, headed there to see how it was looking. From sea level, however, it was a bit disappointing but I had noted a small road leading up away from the beach over a hill and decided to take a look at that.

Technical Details
Medium-format SLR Camera with a 55mm wide-angle lens, and Kodak Ektachrome 64.

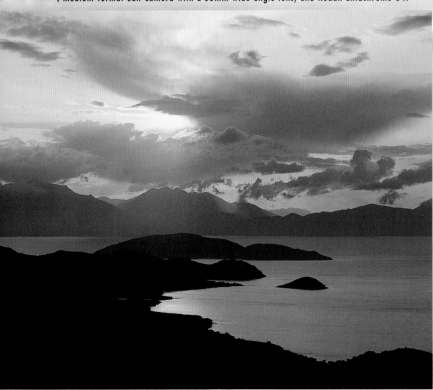

This photograph was taken on the south coast of Crete some time after the sun had set. The much lower contrast and more muted colours have produced a gentler, more romantic image than the previous picture. It's always worth waiting for a while after the sun has set, as this is often when some of the more interesting colour effects are created.

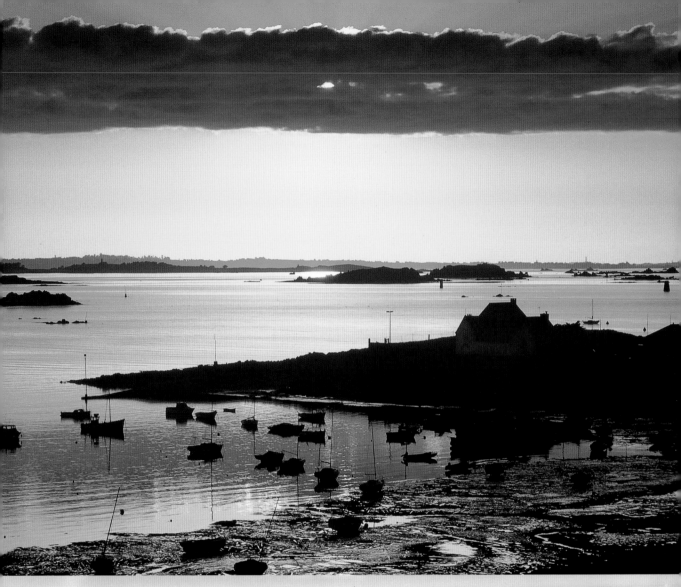

Acting

Although I had not climbed very high the scene took on a very **different aspect** and I liked the way the sunlight was creating a rich **texture** on the wet sand and rippled water. My intention was to wait until the sun was on the point of setting but when it momentarily **went behind** a small cloud bank the time seemed right and I shot this picture. Although I took others just before and after the sunset none of the resulting pictures had this beautiful **golden quality**.

Technical Details

Medium-format SLR Camera with a 55–110mm zoom lens and Fuji Velvia.

Rule of Thumb

Calculating the exposure for sunsets can be tricky, especially when areas of the sky are very bright and when the sun itself is in the frame. A useful technique is to take a reading from the sky above or to one side of the brightest area, making sure that none of this is included. It is also always wise to bracket your exposure to at least one stop over and one stop under when using transparency film.

Magic of Light

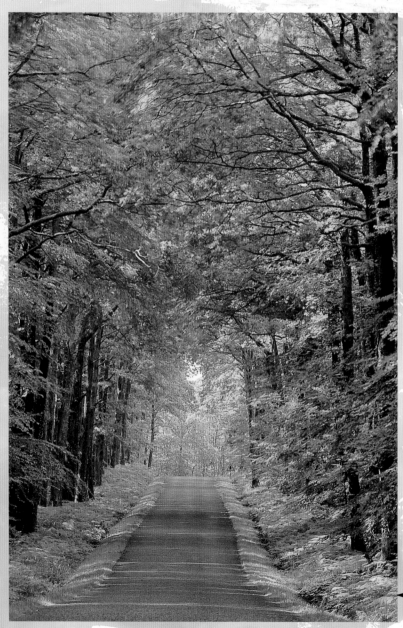

Seeing

This was one of those **opportunist** pictures that crop up now and then. I was staying at a small hotel in North Devon, UK, during the winter and woke early. On looking out I was saddened to see a **grey, cloudy sky** which threatened a rather wet day ahead. Suddenly, however, a **shaft of sunlight** lit the cliff beside the small bay in a very **dramatic way**.

Thinking

I could not get to my camera **fast** enough as I sensed that this gap in the cloud would **quickly close**. The sun was so low that most of the rocky beach was **in shadow** and I needed to use a long-focus lens in order to **exclude** as much of the shadow as possible.

This small road leads through the Forest of Orleans in the Loire region of France. I took this photograph in the early summer when the leaves were still a fresh, delicate green and not yet too dense. This has allowed the sunlight to penetrate the foliage and create an attractive dappled effect as well as making the leaves look translucent. I used a viewpoint in the centre of the road so it led directly away into the centre of the image, and used a long-focus lens to frame a relatively small area of the scene. I used both a polarising filter to increase the colour saturation of the foliage and a warm-up filter to enhance the fresh, green colour of the leaves.

▶ Technical Details

35mm SLR Camera with a 75–300mm zoom lens, 81B warm-up and polarising filters, and Fuji Velvia.

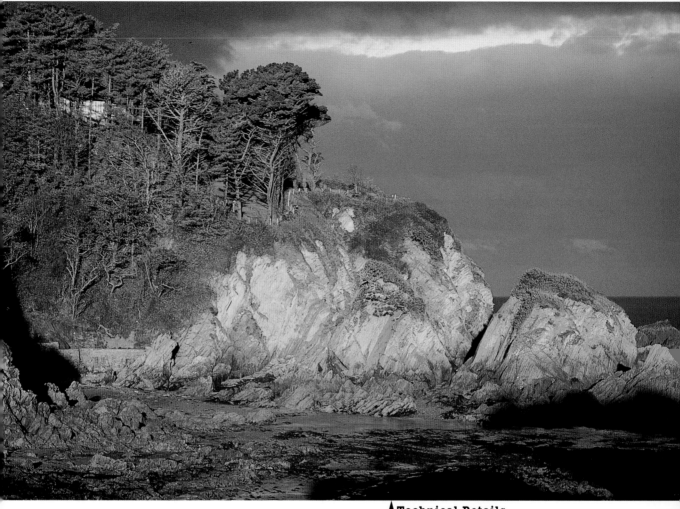

▲ **Technical Details**
35mm SLR Camera with a 70–210mm zoom lens and Fuji Velvia.

Acting

I had left the tripod in my car and was concerned that I might suffer camera shake, so I braced the camera against the edge of the window and framed the image so that all the sunlit area of the scene was included, as well as the lighter band of cloud above the cliff.

Rule of Thumb

You can learn to judge the effect of light more easily if you make a habit of looking at the shadows in a scene. See if they are dense or weak, large or small or if they have sharp or soft edges. The amount and density of shadow in an image will have a big effect on the contrast of an image. Too much contrast will make a picture harsh and unappealing while too little contrast will make it seem flat and dull.

Magic of Light

Seeing

This almost biblical scene was at the Pushkar camel fair. A small town on the edge of India's province of Rajasthan, and an important place of pilgrimage for Hindus, it hosts this massive country fair each November, where hundreds of thousands of people and animals descend on the town and turn the surrounding sand dunes into a vast, tented suburb.

Thinking

This was just one of three wonderful days when I could hardly bear to put my camera down and encountered photogenic situations at every turn. I was, however, anxious to capture the scene as the day drew to a close, but the sunsets had been non-events, as the haze and smoke from thousands of camp fires made the sun disappear quite early. On this occasion though, there was a pleasing orange glow in the sky.

Acting

I first tried shooting with a long focal-length lens to frame the silhouetted camels on the brow of the distant hill, with the sun appearing much larger in proportion. The problem was that there were quite a few other keen photographers around, and although they were silhouetted they were nonetheless very obvious, especially some standing near the distant group of camels. In the end, I found using a wider-angle lens and including foreground details was a more satisfactory approach.

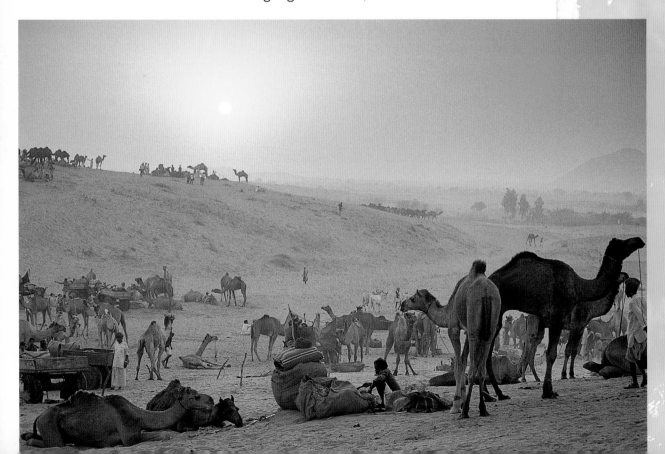

Technical Details
35mm SLR Camera with a 35–70mm zoom lens and Fuji Velvia.

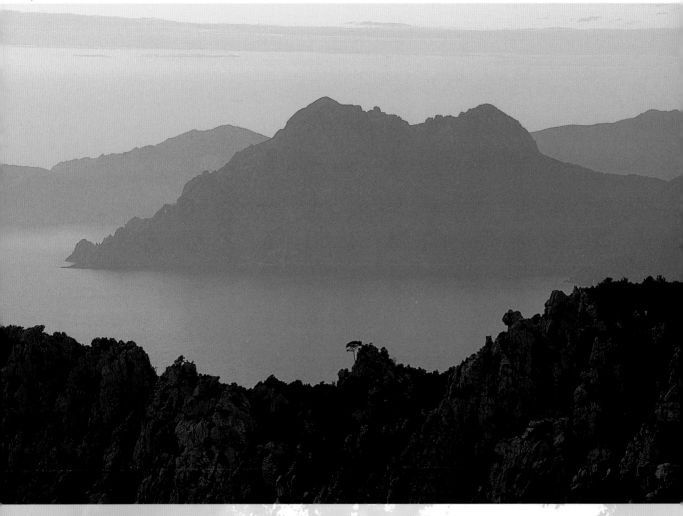

The location for this photograph is the Bay of Porto on the French island of Corsica. This viewpoint is near the village of Piana which is known for the nearby rock formations called Les Calanches. I'd chosen this position in order to photograph the dramatic red rocks at sunset, which are in the foreground of this picture, but waited to see what might develop after the sun had set. I was delighted to find the scene had been transformed into one of soft, pastel pinks and blues, a complete contrast to the scene only a short while earlier.

Rule of Thumb

Judging the density of shadows and the overall contrast of an image can be made easier by viewing it through half-closed eyes or with the lens of an SLR stopped down to a small aperture.

Technical Details
35mm SLR Camera with a 35–70mm zoom lens and Fuji Provia.

Using Daylight

It is often the quality of light which distinguishes a powerful and evocative image from a simple snapshot. Modern cameras, lenses and films make it possible to take photographs successfully in light so poor it would be difficult to read a book. The quantity of light falling on a subject is seldom a problem now but its quality remains an elusive factor.

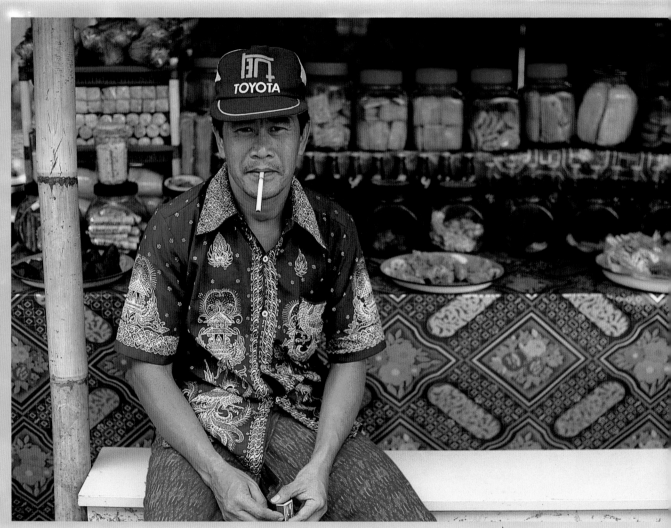

location
Street market - Bali

↑ Technical Details
35mm Single Lens Reflex - 35-70mm lens, Fuji Velvia.

Seeing

I saw this group of sari-clad ladies standing in a small street near a market. But the very bright sunlight tended to create a rather muddled and jarring quality.

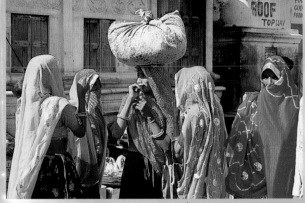

↑ Technical Details
35mm Single Lens Reflex - 75-300mm zoom lens, Fuji Provia.

Acting

My subjects looked settled in their conversation so I had time to take a slow walk around them and from this viewpoint I found that the sun was lighting them in a way which picked out the most dominant colours and the highlights created interesting shapes. From here, they were also placed in front of a shaded area of background which helped to simplify the image. I used my zoom lens to frame the shot in a way which isolated the most effective part of the scene and also cropped out the more distracting highlights and colours.

Thinking

I felt that if I could find a viewpoint from which the almost overhead sunlight created a better balance of light and shade it could produce a pleasing image.

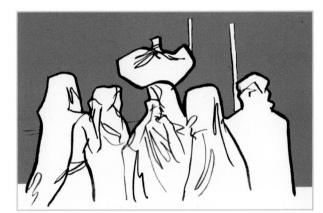

Rule of Thumb

A potential problem with sunlight is that it can often create too much contrast, especially with subjects which are highly detailed or filled with bold colours, like this street scene for instance. The softer light of an overcast day can be far more sympathetic for situations like these. On a sunny day they have to be approached with care if muddled and jarring images are to be avoided. As a gereral rule it's best not to centre the subject in the frame. This image shows how a more effective composition can be created with careful framing.

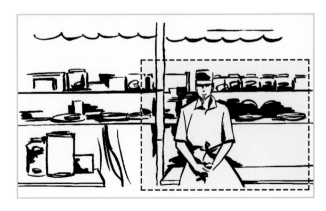

Dawn, Dusk & Sunset

Staying up late and getting up early are two of the best ways of increasing your chances of taking pictures which stand out from the crowd. Not necessarily for the sake of a sunrise or sunset, dusk and dawn can create some quite subtle and beautiful effects even on a cloudy day. However, it's vital to know precisely where to go, it's no good getting up at 4.00 am and then driving round looking for something to photograph, this is a recipe for frustration and disappointment.

Technical Details
35mm Single Lens Reflex - 35-70mm zoom lens, neutral - graduated filter, Fuji Velvia.

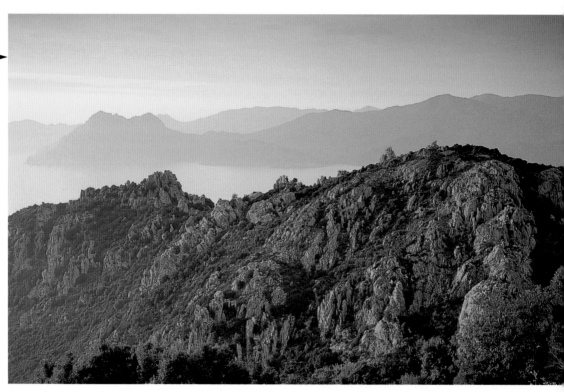

location
Les Calanches - Piana, Corsica

Rule of Thumb

As well as providing a striking quality of light, working at unsociable hours is also a useful way of photographing popular tourist spots which can be swarming with people during the normal hours. Few holidaymakers are prepared to miss breakfast and, up until around 9.00 am, you can often have the place to yourself. Quite apart from it being easier to take photographs at such times, there's something quite magical about places like this mosque before the crowds arrive.

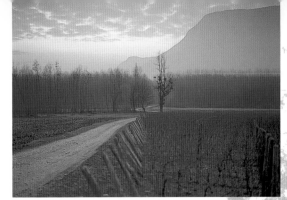

Seeing

This rock formation is a very striking feature of the Corsican coastline and they are, naturally, a very rich red-rust colour. I first saw them on a dull misty day and the dramatic appearance shown in this picture simply wasn't there.

Thinking

I felt that the most powerful effect would be created when the sun was itself quite red in the early morning or the late evening. But I also wanted to show the rocks with the sea in the background and this dictated the time of day - late evening.

Acting

Finding the best viewpoint was the most important part of shooting the picture and I spent an hour or so during the afternoon doing this. All that remained was to set up my camera and tripod and simply wait until the sun became low enough in the sky to create a really warm light. I used a neutral graduated filter to help retain some tone and colour in the sky.

location
Jami Masjid Mosque - Old Delhi India

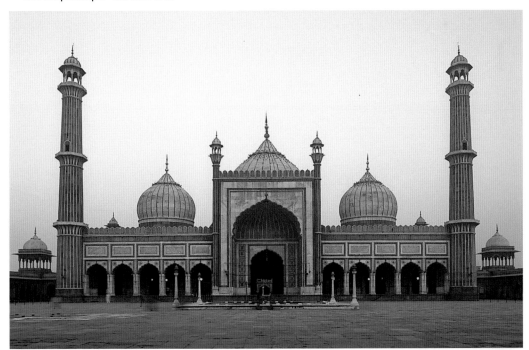

Technical Details
6x4.5cm Single Lens Reflex - 55mm lens, neutral-graduated filter, 5 seconds at f8, Fuji Velvia.

Technical Details
35mm Single Lens Reflex - 28mm shift lens, Fuji Velvia.

Dawn, Dusk & Sunset

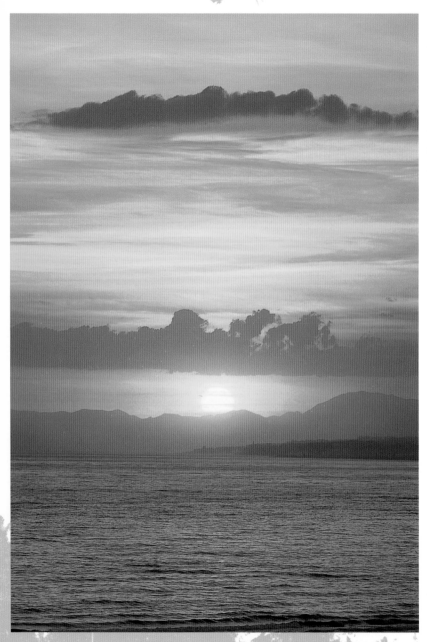

Rule of Thumb

When taking an exposure reading for a sunset a useful tip is to aim the camera just above or to one side of the brightest area of sky, where the sun itself is, and to make sure it is excluded from the reading. It is advisable to bracket your exposures when using transparency film giving a stop or so more and less than the indicated exposure in increments of one third or half a stop.

Technical Details
6x4.5cm Single Lens Reflex - 50mm lens, neutral-graduated filter, Fuji Velvia.

Technical Details
6x4.5cm Single Lens Reflex - 105-210 zoom lens, neutral-graduated filter, Fuji Velvia.

location
Costa del Sol near Nerja - Andalucia, Spain

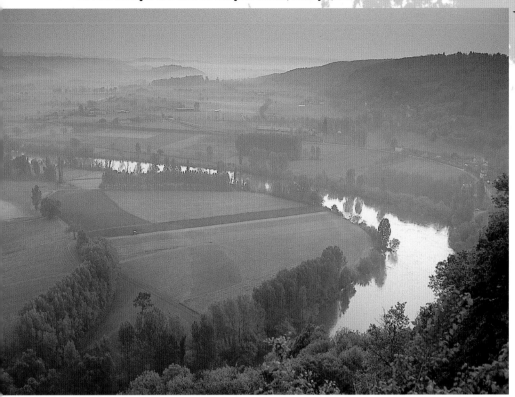

Technical Details
35mm Single Lens Reflex
- 35-70mm zoom lens,
neutral-graduated filter,
Fuji Velvia.

This shot was taken looking towards the east just as the sun was beginning to rise. Because the landscape was much darker than the bright sky I used a neutral graduated filter to enable me to give enough exposure to record detail in the foreground without overexposing the sky.

Seeing

I found this viewpoint in the evening and it afforded a very good view of the monastery, the sun was behind the mountain and the lighting was quite interesting but the building itself was rather silhouetted.

Thinking

It occurred to me that the very first rays of the sun the following morning might create a very striking effect as they illuminated the monastery building.

Acting

I made sure that I was in the same spot the next morning well before the hour of sunrise and had my camera set ready on the tripod for that first glow of light. I used a graduated filter to make the sky a little darker.

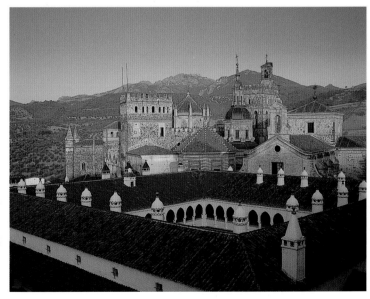

location
The Monastery of Guadalupe - Extramadura, Spain

Bad Weather

The majority of travel photographs are shot in sunlight for the very obvious reason that such images tend to look more inviting. But shooting in bad weather can have very positive advantages as the resulting photographs will often have a more eye-catching and atmospheric quality.

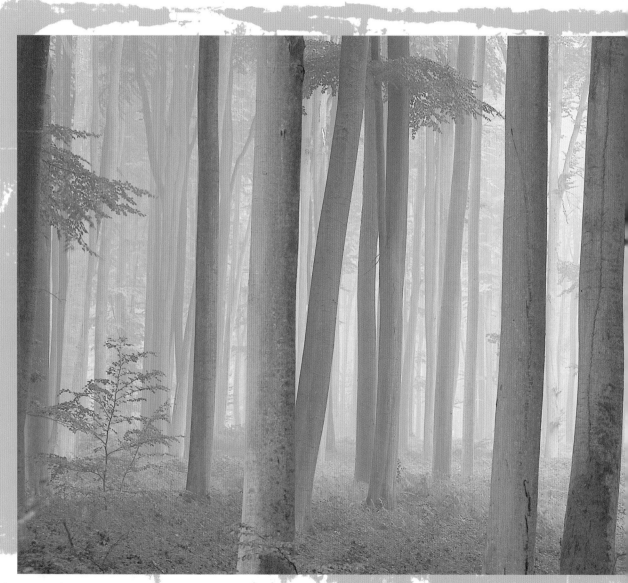

location
The Forest of Lyons - Normandy, France

Technical Details
6x4.5cm Single Lens Reflex - 300mm
lens, 81B warm-up filter, 1 sec at
f22, Fuji Velvia.

location
Dovedale - Cumbria, UK

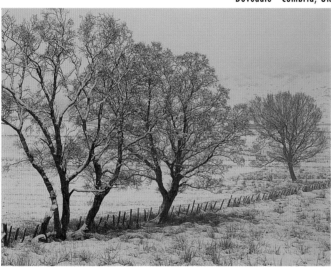

Technical Details
6x4.5cm Single Lens Reflex -
55-110 zoom lens, Fuji Velvia.

Seeing

On this morning, the countryside of
Normandy was blanketed in a thick fog
and it seemed as if there was little chance
of doing any photography. But driving
through this forest revealed a most
atmospheric scene with the
potential to produce some strong images.

Thinking

I felt that the most striking quality of the scene was the
strange juxtaposition of shapes created by
the tree trunks and this altered very significantly
as I changed the camera viewpoint and as the
mist swirled through the forest.

Acting

I walked slowly into the forest looking for the most
effective arrangement of shapes often
moving only a foot or so to obtain a very different
effect. This was, I felt, one of the most successful
images and I used a 300mm lens to isolate a
small section of the scene, which
accentuated the effect of the fog.

Dramatic Skies

The sky can be a very important element of many photographs. As a general rule, if it doesn't make a positive contribution to the image, when there is a blank white sky on an overcast day for instance, it's best, where possible, to exclude it altogether. But even when the sky is interesting there are a number of things you can do to maximise its effect.

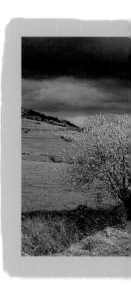

Seeing

It was the single, isolated tree set in this bleak rocky landscape which first caught my eye and it was not until I began to set up my camera that I noticed the approach of the small white cloud.

Thinking

I realised that if I could find the right viewpoint quickly, anticipating where the cloud would go, I could have a much stronger image than the one I had planned to shoot.

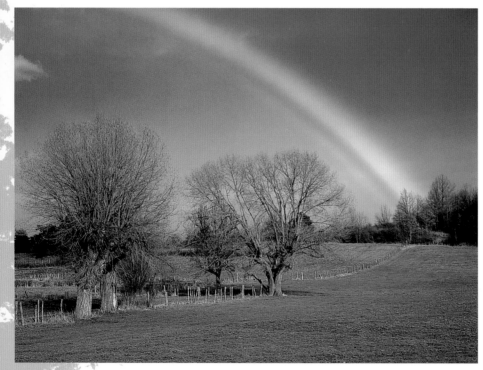

location
Near Issoire - Auvergne, France

Acting

I fitted a polarising filter to obtain the maximum contrast between the cloud and blue sky and fitted a long-focus lens to exclude all but the tree and cloud, using an upright format. At the last moment I also decided to use a neutral graduated filter to make the very top section of the sky and cloud a little darker.

location
The Serrania de Ronda - Andalucia, Spain

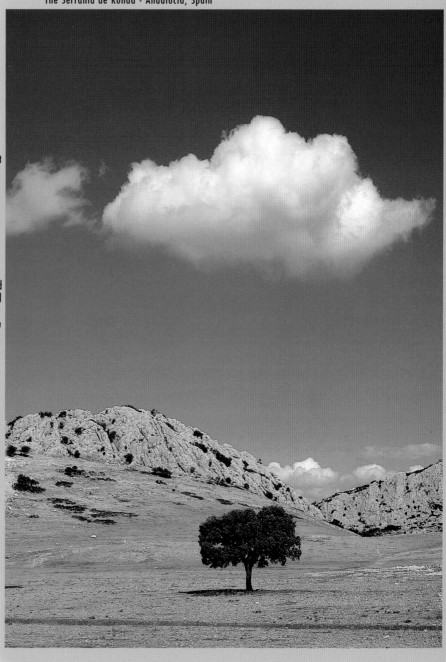

location
Near Clermont Ferrand, Auvergne, France

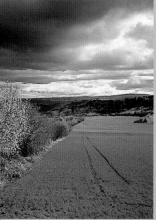

A graduated filter is invaluable for making the most of dark, brooding skies since they will often record lighter than appears visually if left unfiltered. This is because the exposure needed to produce a full range of tones and detail in the foreground will usually result in the sky being overexposed.

Technical Details ↑
6x4.5cm Single Lens Reflex - 50mm lens, neutral-graduated and 81C warm-up filters, Fuji Velvia.

Technical Details
6x4.5cm Single Lens Reflex - 55-110 zoom lens, 81B warm-up filter, Fuji Velvia.

Technical Details →
6x4.5cm Single Lens Reflex - 105-210 zoom lens, polarising, 81C warm-up and neutral graduated filters, Fuji Velvia.

Dramatic Skies

location
Near San Sebastian - Guipuzcoa, Spain

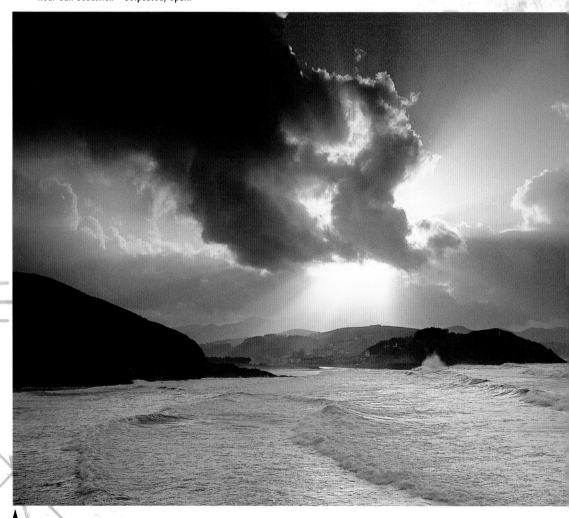

Technical Details
35mm Single Lens Reflex - 24mm lens,
81C warm up and neutral-graduated filters,
Fuji Velvia.

location
Win Green, near Shaftesbury, Wiltshire, UK

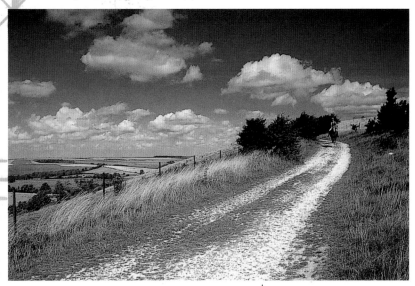

Technique

A graduated filter is most often used so that the line of graduation runs parallel to the horizon but with a square filter system they can be used at any angle, even upside down to make a foreground darker for instance. They can be especially useful when photographing a deep blue sky with a polariser when it has an uneven effect, a problem often encountered when using a wide angle lens. In such cases, like this summer landscape, the graduated filter can be used at an angle over one or other corner of the sky area to make it more even.

Technical Details
35mm Single Lens Reflex - 24mm lens, 81C warm-up, polarising and neutral graduated-filters, Fuji Velvia.

Available Light

Dark is a relative term, there are few outdoor situations where there is no light at all and it's quite possible to shoot pictures in moonlight with a long enough exposure if the subject is static and you use a tripod. When people are involved, or the subject is moving, the temptation is to use flash when the light is poor but this can easily destroy the atmosphere of a scene and making the most of the available light can be a better option.

Seeing

The atmosphere of a grape-pickers lunch is a lively one and this room in which they gathered was very large and poorly lit, but I felt that these qualities were essential to the picture.

Thinking

The room was simply too large to even consider the use of flash so I had to look for ways in which I could get a manageable exposure using the existing light, weak daylight filtering through small windows near the eaves.

Acting

This particular viewpoint allowed me to shoot towards one of the strongest light sources and a reflection it created on one of the tables. This gave the otherwise dark and shadowy scene a good area of highlight. I simply used the fastest film I had with me, set the widest aperture on my lens and waited for a moment when the people in the immediate foreground were fairly still before shooting at the necessary half a second shutter speed.

location
The refractory
of Chateau
Lascombes,
Margaux -
Gironde, France

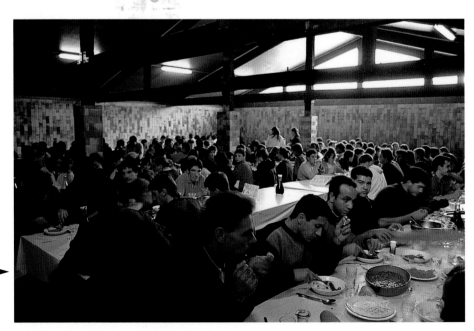

Technical Details
35mm Single Lens Reflex -
35-70mm zoom lens,
1/2 sec at f2.8,
Fuji Provia ISO 400.

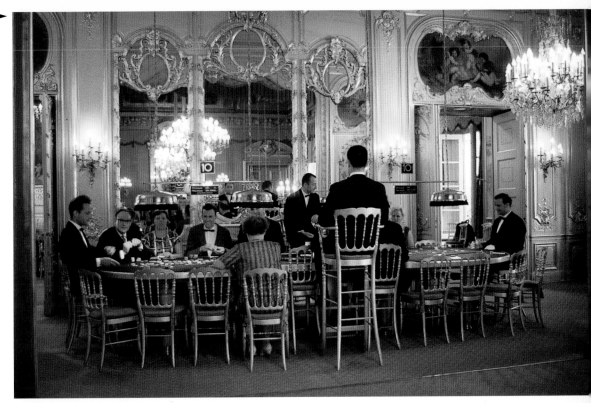

Technical Details
35mm Single Lens Reflex - 35mm lens, 1/4 sec at f2.8, Kodak High Speed Ektachrome.

location
The Casino - Baden Baden - Germany

location
A Fromagerie
in Montmartre -
Paris, France

Technical Details
35mm Rangefinder Camera - 28mm lens,
1/60 sec at f2.8, Kodak E100 SW rated at ISO 200.

Rule of Thumb

The commonest problem when shooting pictures in available light is that of excessive contrast. You can do a great deal to avoid this by choosing viewpoints and framing your images in ways which excludes both the brightest highlights and the densest shadows.

Available Light

Seeing

I wanted to take a shot of the Christmas tree before it became completely dark but the illuminations were not switched on until all the light had gone from the sky.

Thinking

I thought that my best approach was to fill the frame with only the illuminated areas of the scene and to include the fountain in the foreground. This helped to make the sky less important and the fact that it recorded as black would then not detract too much from the picture.

Acting

I used a very close viewpoint and the long end of my medium range zoom to frame the image quite tightly. Although, by now, the scene was lit almost completely by artificial light I opted to use daylight film because I wanted the image to have a warm, golden quality.

Rule of Thumb

When shooting pictures of illuminated buildings or streets at night it is best to try and shoot before all the light goes out of the sky. This will help to reduce the contrast of the image, providing more shadow detail, and will allow the outlines of the buildings to be seen more clearly.

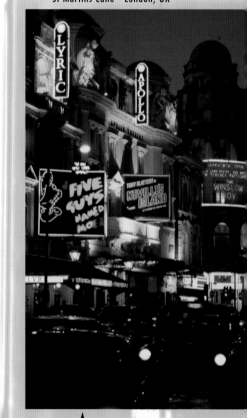

location
St Martins Lane - London, UK

Technical Details
35mm Single Lens Reflex - 35-70mm zoom lens,
1/4 sec at f2.8, Fuji Provia.

Technical
Details
35mm Single
Lens Reflex -
35-70mm
zoom lens,
1/2 sec at f4,
Fuji Provia.

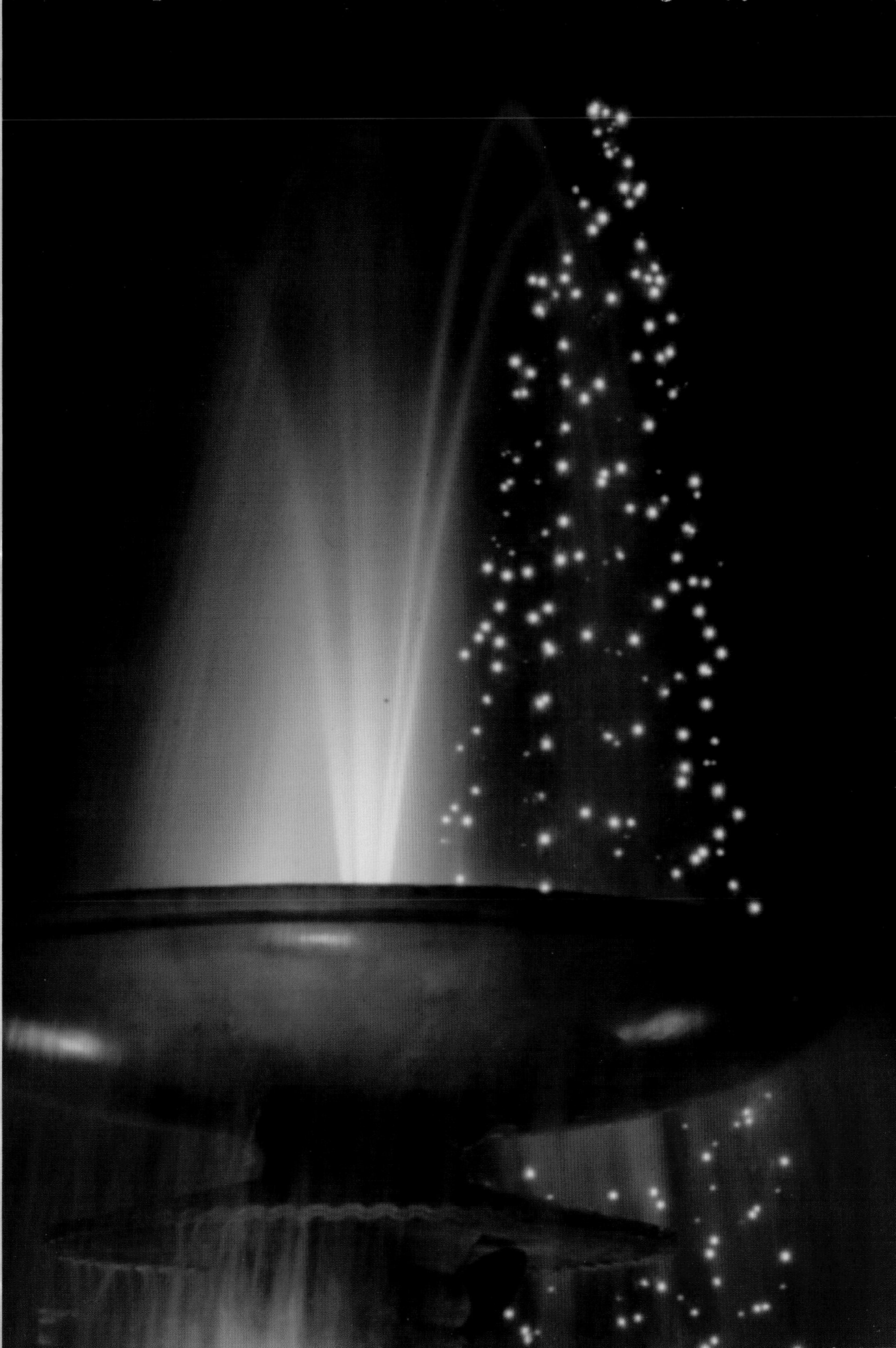

location
Trafalgar
Square -
London, UK

Flash Photography

Flash has the drawback that it's not possible to actually
see the effect of the lighting until your film is processed. This means you need to think about the way it's
being aimed quite carefully in order to make an educated guess at it's effect.

Seeing
The situation had considerable potential, I thought, but it
depended upon seeing something of the extent of the
vast cellar and its countless bottles and also of the
action of the man who was turning them, an
important technique in Champagne production.

Thinking
Flash alone would have resulted in the more distant area
of the cellar being a black abyss, whereas an
available light shot would have resulted in the
man being largely in silhouette.

Technical Details
35mm Single Lens Reflex - 35-70mm zoom lens,
1/4 sec at f4 with fill-in flash, Fuji Provia.

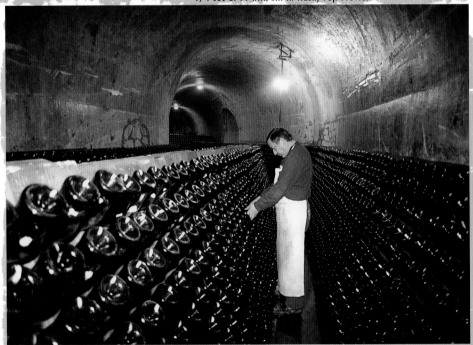

location
The Cellars of Moet et Chandon, Reims - Champagne Ardenne, France

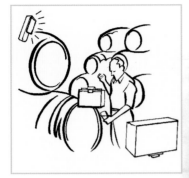

This cellar had virtually no ambient light so I was obliged to use flash exclusively. I set up one flash behind the subject to light the stream of wine and the background barrels and another to one side of the camera, diffused with a soft box, to light the man.

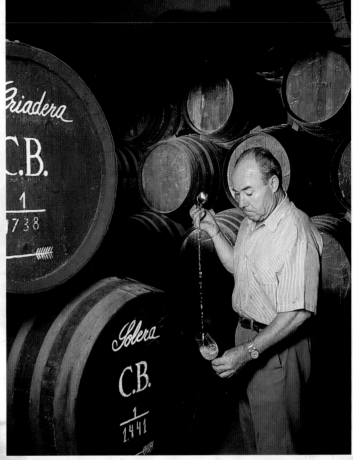

Technical Details
6x4.5cm Single Lens Reflex -
55-110mm zoom lens,
two flash units at f5.6,
Fuji Provia.

Acting

I took an exposure reading for the **ambient** light and set the necessary shutter speed and aperture. I then adjusted the power of the flash to give a half stop less than the strictly correct exposure for the **flash** exposure, to avoid the effect appearing too artificial.

Rule of Thumb

The most common fault with flash-on-camera shots is that of not allowing for the quite dramatic drop in light intensity as it travels further from the gun. This can be avoided by making sure the distance from the camera to the subject is always more than that between the subject and the background, preferably at least double.

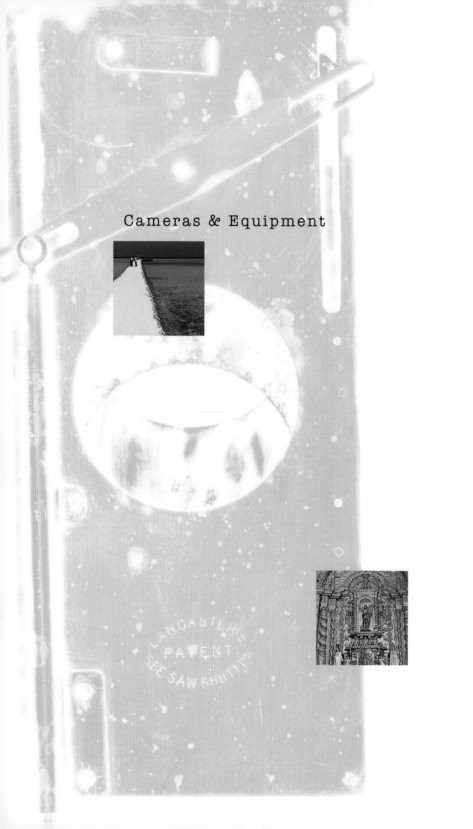

Cameras & Equipment

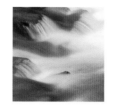

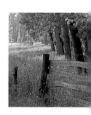

LANCASTER'S
PATENT
SEE SAW SHUTTER

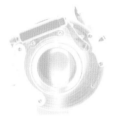

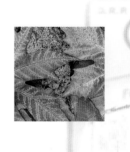

4

Your choice of equipment will depend on
what you want out of your camera,
whether you wish to sell your work, which subjects you are likely to choose and
how much you can afford to spend. Some items are useful whatever subjects you
photograph while others have limited, specialist use.

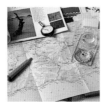

Choosing a Camera

Formats

Image size is the most basic consideration. The image area of a 35mm camera is approximately 24x36mm but with roll film it can be from 45x60mm up to 60x90mm according to camera choice. The degree of enlargement needed to provide, say, an A4 reproduction is much less for a roll film format than for 35mm and gives a potentially higher image quality.

For most photographers the choice is between 35mm, APS and 120 roll film cameras. APS offers a slightly smaller format than 35mm and for images larger than 6x9cm it is necessary to use a view camera of 5x4in or 10x8in format.

Pros & Cons

APS cameras have a more limited choice of film types and accessories and are designed primarily for the use of colour negative film. 35mm SLR cameras have the widest range of film types and accessories and provide the best compromise between image quality, size, weight and cost of equipment. Both accessories and film costs are significantly more expensive with roll film cameras, and the range of lenses and accessories more limited than with 35mm equipment.

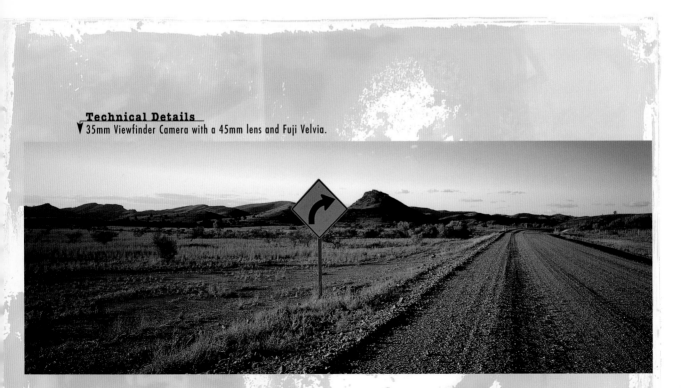

Technical Details
▼ 35mm Viewfinder Camera with a 45mm lens and Fuji Velvia.

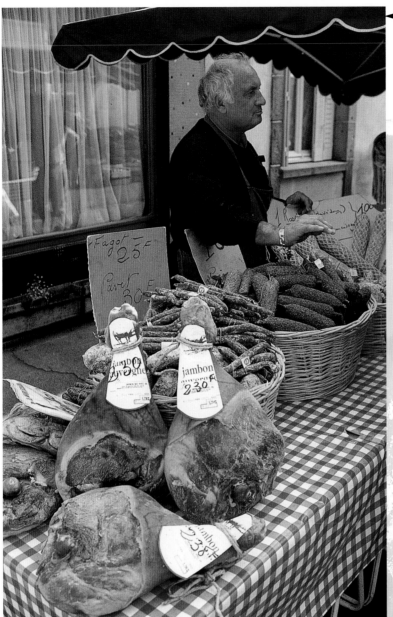

Technical Details

35mm SLR Camera with a 24–85mm zoom lens, an 81A warm-up filter and Kodak Ektachrome 100 SW.

I used my 35mm SLR for this picture taken in a French market but it is the type of subject which can be handled equally well with a 35mm viewfinder or compact camera.

Waterproof and Underwater Cameras

It's possible to buy cameras which can be used underwater to a considerable depth, for serious sub-aqua photography, or simpler models which are waterproof and also capable of being taken a few metres under the surface. These can be an ideal choice for those who wish to use their camera to photograph water sports or for a situation such as a beach, without fear of water or sand damage.

Digital Cameras

These are now a feasible alternative to film cameras, as one or two million pixel resolution can produce ink-jet prints up to 7x5in, comparable in quality to those from a photolab. Digital cameras have an advantage in that the results can be seen immediately and assessed, allowing the option to reject bad results and re-shoot straight away. The disadvantage is that the storage capacity of images at high resolution is quite limited.

This shot of The Australian Outback was taken on a special panoramic camera. Many more simple cameras have an optional panoramic setting, the APS system for instance, which can help to produce a more pleasing composition with some subjects.

Camera Types

There are two basic choices between Roll Film, 35mm and APS Cameras; the Viewfinder or Rangefinder Camera and the Single Lens Reflex, or SLR.

Pros & Cons

An SLR allows you to view through the taking lens and to see the actual image which will be recorded on the film, but the viewfinder camera uses a separate optical system. This can be a major disadvantage with close-up photography in particular, as an optical viewfinder becomes increasingly inaccurate as the camera is moved closer to the subject.

In addition, the whole image appears in focus when seen through a viewfinder camera but the effect of focusing can be seen on the screen of an SLR, making it possible to more accurately judge the depth of field. It is also much easier to judge and control the effect of filters, such as polarisers and neutral graduates when using an SLR.

Generally, facilities like autofocus and exposure control are more accurate and convenient with SLR cameras and you can see the effect of filters and attachments. SLR cameras have a much wider range of accessories and lenses available to them and are more suited to subjects like wild life when very long-focus lenses are needed. Viewfinder cameras, such as the Leica or Mamiya 7, tend to be lighter and quieter than their equivalent SLRs, but they are not ideally suited to close-up photography because of the limitations of the viewing system.

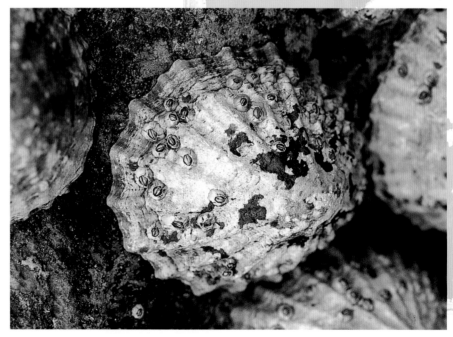

For this close-up of a limpet shell I used a 35mm SLR with a macro lens.

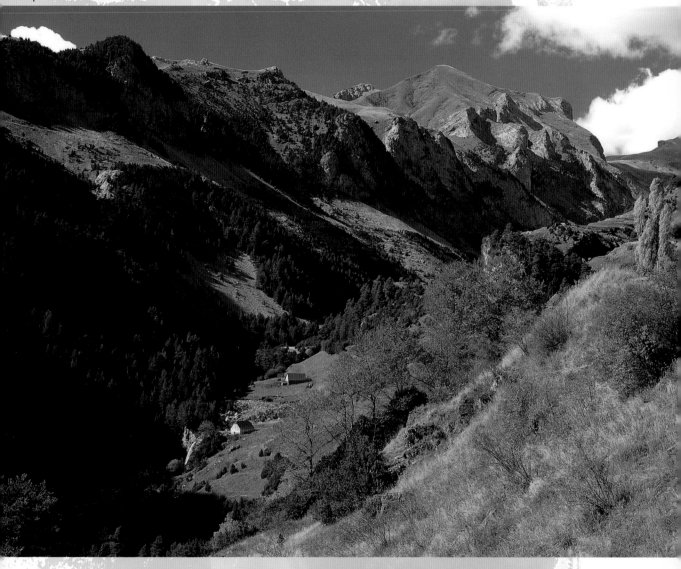

I used my medium-format camera for this landscape, photographed in the Spanish Pyrenees near the town of Bielsa. The additional degree of sharpness and tonal quality of the larger format over 35mm can be an advantage with this type of subject, especially when the image is reproduced very large.

Choosing Lenses

A **standard lens** is one which creates a field of view of about 45° and has a focal length equivalent to the diagonal measurement of the film format i.e. **50mm, with a 35mm** camera and **80mm with a 6x6cm** camera. Lenses with a shorter focal length create a **wider field** of view and those with a longer focal length produce a narrower field of view. **Zoom lenses** provide a wide range of focal lengths within a single optic, taking up less space and offering more convenience than having several **fixed lenses**.

Pros & Cons

Many ordinary zooms have a maximum aperture of f5.6 or smaller. This can be quite restricting when **fast shutter speeds** are needed in low light levels and a fixed focal-length lens with a **wider maximum aperture** of f2.8 or f4 can sometimes be a better choice. **Zoom lenses** are available for most 35mm SLR cameras over a wide range of focal lengths but it's important to appreciate that the **image quality** will be lower with lenses which are designed to cover more than about a **three to one ratio**, i.e. 28–85mm or 70–210mm.

Special Lenses

A lens of more than 300mm will seldom be necessary for the majority of photographic subjects, but one between **400mm and 600mm** is often necessary to obtain close-up images of subjects, such as sports, wild animals and birds. **Extenders** can allow you to increase the focal length of an existing lens; a x1.4 extender will make a 200mm lens into 300mm and a x2 extender to 400mm. There will be some **loss of sharpness** with all but the most expensive optics and a **reduction in maximum aperture** of one and two stops respectively.

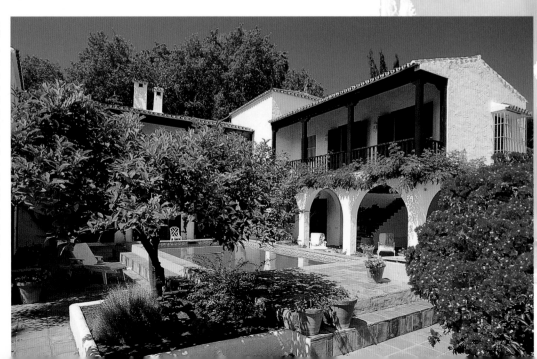

Using a wide-angle lens for this picture of a holiday villa in Spain has enabled me to include the bougainvillea in the close foreground as well as all of the house and the tree on the left-hand side. This has helped to give the image a three-dimensional quality, as well as showing the villa in the context of its setting. I used a small aperture to obtain maximum depth of field.

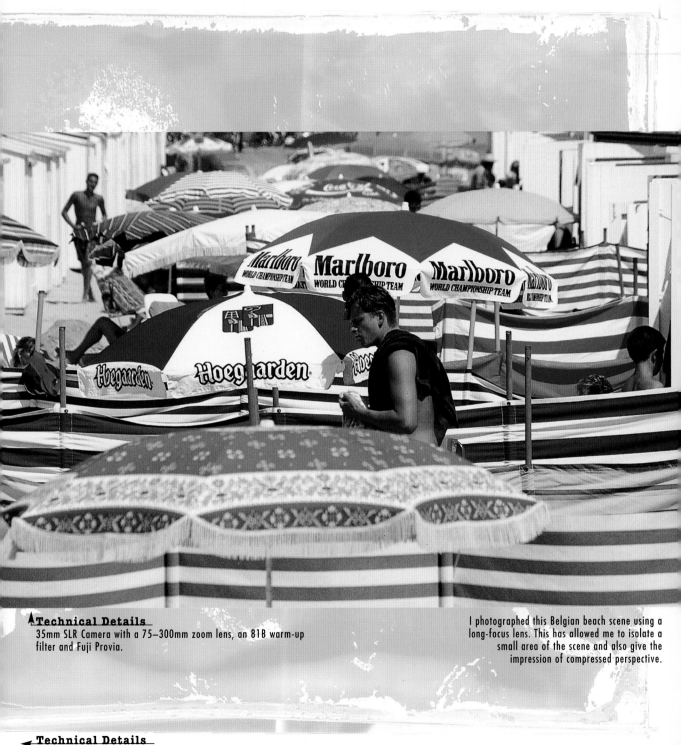

Technical Details
35mm SLR Camera with a 75–300mm zoom lens, an 81B warm-up filter and Fuji Provia.

I photographed this Belgian beach scene using a long-focus lens. This has allowed me to isolate a small area of the scene and also give the impression of compressed perspective.

Technical Details
35mm SLR Camera with a 20mm wide-angle lens, 81C warm-up and polarising filters, and Fuji Velvia.

Camera Accessories

There are a wide range of accessories which can be used to control the image and increase the camera's capability.

Extension tubes, bellows units and dioptre lenses will all allow the lens to be focused at a closer distance than it's designed for.

A selection of filters will help to extend the degree of control over the colour quality of an image and a square filter system, such as Cokin or HiTech, is by far the most convenient and practical option. These allow the same filters to be used with all your lenses regardless of the size of the lens mounts, as each can be fitted with an adapter upon which the filter-holder itself can be easily slipped on and off.

Technical Details
35mm SLR Camera with a 24–85mm zoom lens, an extension tube and Fuji Velvia.

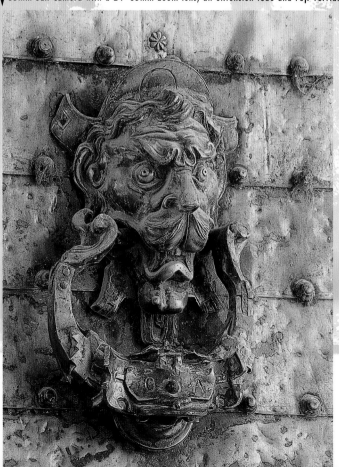

A polarising filter is extremely useful for reducing the brightness of reflections in non-metallic surfaces, such as foliage, and will also make a blue sky record as a richer blue, creating greater relief with white clouds.

Polarisers are available in either linear or circular form. The former can interfere with some auto-focusing and exposure systems. Your camera's instruction book should tell you, but if in doubt use a circular polariser.

Technique
A soft-focus filter can be effective in some circumstances to reduce contrast and colour saturation and help create a more romantic mood for subjects such as portraits and landscapes.

Technique
A tripod should be considered obligatory whenever it is possible to use one as it enables you to aim, frame and focus the camera on your subject with the knowledge that it will remain accurately positioned. This allows you to concentrate more on matters like composition and lighting.

A photograph like this close-up shot of a detail of the cathedral door in Cordoba, Spain, needed an extension tube or bellows unit to enable a normal lens to focus at a close enough distance.

Rule of Thumb
It's best to buy the most substantial tripod you feel able to carry comfortably, as a very lightweight one can be of limited usefulness. A shake-free means of firing the camera, such as a cable release or a remote trigger, is advisable when using a tripod-mounted camera.

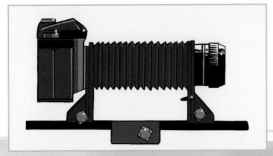

This diagram shows an extension tube fitted between the camera body and lens.

Rule of Thumb

Perhaps one of the most important accessories which can significantly improve your photography is a tripod, as it can greatly improve image sharpness. The effects of camera shake are much more noticeable when the subject is close to the camera and small apertures are often needed to create sufficient depth of field; a tripod allows slower shutter speeds to be used without risk. A tripod is also extremely useful when you wish to include yourself in a picture using the camera's delay setting.

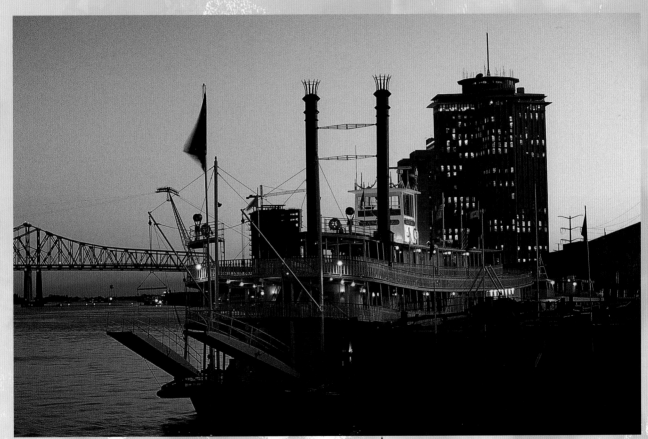

Technique

A Polaroid back can be bought to fit many professional roll film and 35mm cameras such as the Canon EOS1N and the Mamiya 645. These can be extremely useful when using flash lighting as the exact effect of the set-up can be seen before the image is exposed onto normal film.

Technical Details

35mm SLR Camera with a 75–300mm zoom lens and Fuji Velvia.

I took this photograph of New Orleans, USA, some time after sunset, by which time it was getting quite dark. I needed an exposure of around one second which made the use of a tripod essential.

Apertures & Shutter Speeds

The aperture is the device which controls the brightness of the image falling upon the film and is indicated by f stop numbers: f2, f2.8, f4, f5.6, f8, f11, f16, f22 and f32. Each step down, from f2.8 to f4 for example, reduces the amount of light reaching the film by 50% and each step up, from f8 to f5.6 for instance, doubles the brightness of the image. The shutter speed settings control the length of times for which the image is allowed to play on the film and, in conjunction with the aperture, control the exposure and quality of the image.

Technique

The choice of shutter speed determines the degree of sharpness with which a moving subject will be recorded. With a fast-moving subject, like an animal running or a bird flying for instance, a shutter speed of 1/1000 sec or less will be needed to obtain a sharp image.

Technique

Choice of aperture also influences the depth of field, which is the distance in front and beyond the point at which the lens is focused. At wide apertures, like f2.8, the depth of field is quite limited making closer and more distant details appear distinctly out of focus. The effect becomes more pronounced as the focal length of the lens increases and as the focusing distance decreases; so with, say, a 200mm lens focused at one metre and an aperture of f2.8 the range of sharp focus will extend only a very short distance in front and behind the subject. The depth of field increases when a smaller aperture is used and when using a short focal length, or wide-angle lens. A camera with a depth of field preview button will allow you to judge the depth of field in the viewfinder.

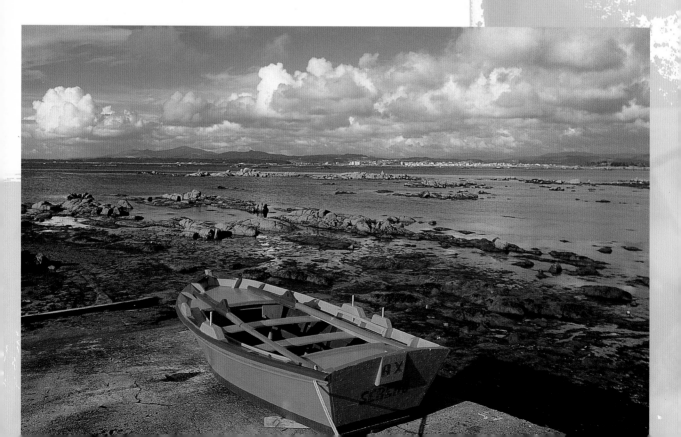

Technical Details
35mm SLR Camera with a 35–70mm zoom lens, 81C warm-up and polarising filters, and Fuji Velvia.

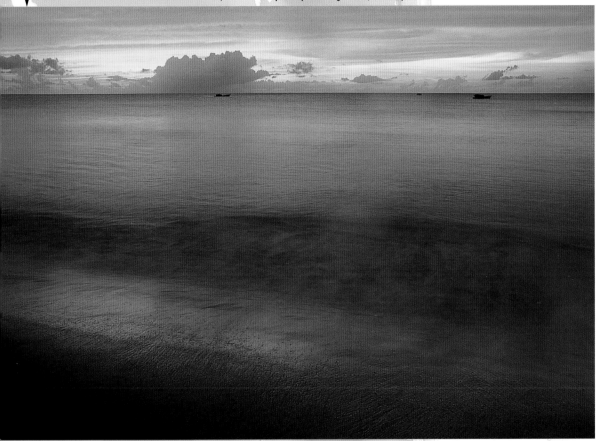

I used a shutter speed of about two seconds to record the moving water as a soft smoke-like blur in this photograph, taken in Tobago, some time after the sun had gone down. A tripod was essential to ensure that the static elements of the image remained sharp.

For this scene, photographed in the Galicia region of Spain, I set a small aperture to ensure that the image was as sharp as possible from the closest to the furthest details.

Technical Details
35mm SLR Camera with a 20–35mm zoom lens, 81C warm-up and polarising filters, and Fuji Velvia.

Rule of Thumb

The choice of shutter speed can also affect the image sharpness of a static subject when the camera is hand-held as even slight camera shake can easily cause the image to be blurred. The effect is more pronounced with long-focus lenses and when shooting close-ups. The safest minimum shutter speed should be considered as reciprocal of the focal length of the lens being used; 1/200 sec with a 200mm lens, for instance.

Understanding Exposure

Modern cameras with automatic exposure systems have made some aspects of achieving good quality images much easier, but no system is infallible and an understanding of how exposure meters work will help to ensure a higher success rate.

An **exposure meter**, whether it's a built-in TTL meter or a separate hand meter works on the principle that the subject it is aimed at is a mid-tone, known as an **18% grey**. In practice, of course, the subject is invariably a **mixture of tones and colours** but the assumption is still that, if mixed together, like so many pots of different-coloured paints, the resulting blend would still be the same 18% grey tone.

With most subjects the reading taken from the whole of the **subject** will produce a satisfactory exposure. But if there are aspects of a subject which are abnormal – when it contains large areas of **very light** or **dark tones**, for example – the reading needs to be modified.

An exposure reading from a snow scene for instance, would, if uncorrected, record the white snow as **grey** on film. In the same way, a reading taken from a very dark subject would result in the image being **too light**.

The exposure needs to be **decreased** when the subject is essentially dark in tone or when there are large **areas of shadow** close to the camera. With abnormal subjects it is often possible to take a close-up or **spot-reading** from an area which is of normal, average tone.

Technical Details
35mm SLR Camera with a 24–85mm zoom lens, 81C warm-up and polarising filters, and Fuji Velvia.

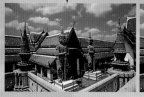
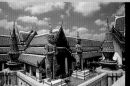
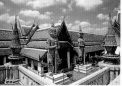
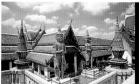
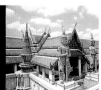

These pictures show the effect of bracketing exposures. The central image received the exposure indicated by the meter while the two darker frames had a third and two thirds of a stop less and the two lighter frames had a third and two thirds of a stop more.

Technique

Many cameras allow you to take a **spot-reading** from a small area of a scene as well as an average reading, and this can be useful for calculating the exposure with subjects of an **abnormal tonal range** or of high contrast. Switching between the average and spot-reading modes is also a good way of **checking** if you are concerned about a potential exposure error. If there is a difference of more than about half a stop, when using transparency film, you need to consider the scene more carefully to decide if a degree of **exposure compensation** is required.

Rule of Thumb

The most common situations in which the exposure taken from a normal average reading needs to be increased are when shooting into the light, when there are large areas of white or very light tones in the scene, when there is a large area of bright sky in the frame and when bright light sources are included in the image, such as a street scene at night.

▲ **Technical Details**
35mm SLR Camera with a 35–70mm zoom lens, 81B warm-up and polarising filters, and Fuji Velvia.

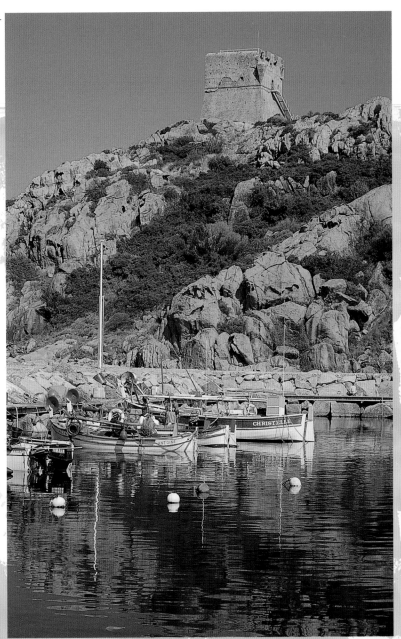

This photograph is of the small harbour of the village of Porto on the French island of Corsica. Being a subject of normal tonal range and contrast, the camera's exposure meter gave me an accurate reading which needed no compensation.

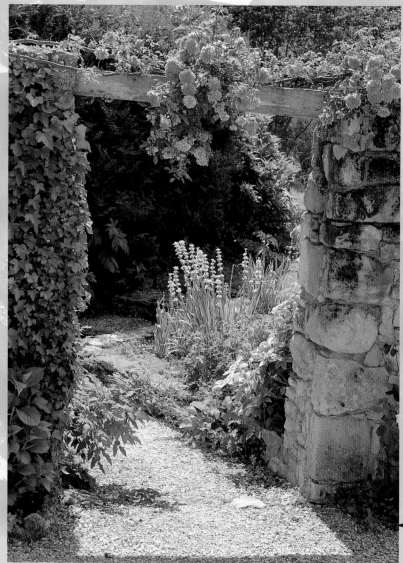

Technique

Clip testing is an effective way of overcoming this problem. For this technique you need to establish your exposure and shoot a complete roll at the **same setting**, assuming the lighting conditions remain the same. You need to allow two frames at the end of the roll, in the case of roll film, or shoot three frames at the beginning of a 35mm film, which you must ask the processing laboratory to **cut off** and process normally. The exposure can then be **judged** and the processing time of the remainder of the film **adjusted** to make the balance of the transparencies lighter or darker if necessary. **Increasing** the effective speed of the film, known as **pushing,** and making the transparency lighter, is more effective than reducing the film speed, known as **pulling,** to make the image darker. For this reason it is best to set your exposure slightly less than calculated if in any doubt.

For this photograph of a garden I gave two-thirds of a stop more exposure than was indicated to compensate for the back-lighting as the exposure meter would have been influenced by the bright highlights and would have indicated less exposure than was really needed. This would have resulted in the shadow tones being too dark and lacking in detail.

Technical Details

Medium-format SLR Camera with a 55–110mm zoom lens, 81C warm-up and polarising filters, and Fuji Velvia.

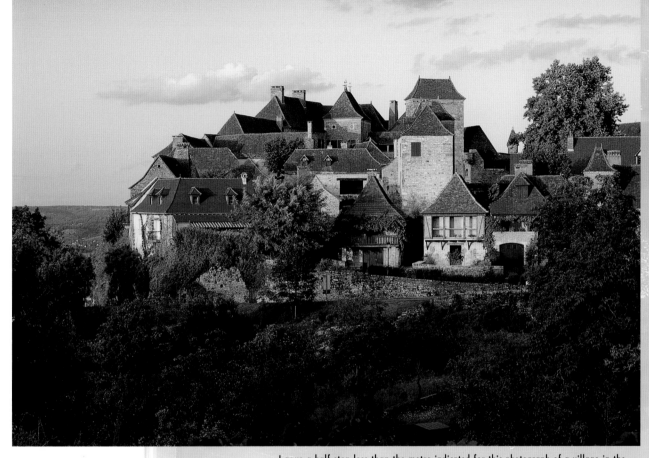

I gave a half stop less than the metre indicated for this photograph of a village in the Dordogne region of France, as the exposure meter would have been influenced by the dark, shadowed foreground and indicated more exposure than was necessary. This would have recorded the sunlit houses as too light a tone.

Technique

Exposure compensation can also be used to alter the quality and effect of an image, especially with transparency film. When a lighter or darker image is required this can be adjusted at the printing stage when shooting on negative film, but with transparency film it must be done at the time the film is exposed.

Rule of Thumb

Although bracketing is effective when dealing with a completely static subject like a landscape or still life it's not always the best solution when taking photographs in situations where the subject is moving, such as when photographing people or animals. Even a slight change in the expression or posture can make one frame very much better than the next and in a bracket this might not be the best exposure.

Choosing Film

There is a huge variety of film types and speeds from which to choose and although, to a degree, it is dependent on personal taste, there are some basic considerations to be made. Unless you wish to achieve special effects through the use of film grain it is generally best to choose a slow, fine-grained film for most colour photography if the subject and lighting conditions permit.

Technical

The choice between colour negative film and transparency film depends partly upon the intended use of the photographs. For book and magazine reproduction, transparency film is universally preferred and transparencies are also demanded by most photo libraries. Transparency film is also necessary for slide presentations. For personal use, and for when colour prints are the main requirement, colour negative film can be a better choice since it has greater exposure latitude and is capable of producing high-quality prints at a lower cost.

Technical

Colour negative film is also the best choice if you are shooting in mixed lighting, or under unknown conditions, such as fluorescent light, as it is more tolerant of colour casts and can be corrected at the printing stage.

Technical

Many films are now produced to suit different subjects such as portraits and landscapes. A warm, strongly saturated film such as Fuji Velvia is ideal for landscapes for example, but does not produce very flattering skin tones.

Technical Details
▼35mm SLR Camera with a 17–35mm zoom lens and Kodak Ektachrome 100 SW.

For this photograph of the cellars of Chateau Lafite Rothschild in France I deliberately used daylight-type film, even though the cellars were lit by artificial lighting; I felt the resulting orange cast would enhance the picture's atmosphere.

Rule of Thumb

With all film types, their speed determines the basic image quality. A slow film of ISO 50, for instance, has finer grain and produces a significantly sharper image than a fast film of, say, ISO 800. The accuracy and saturation of the colours will also be superior when using films with a lower ISO rating.

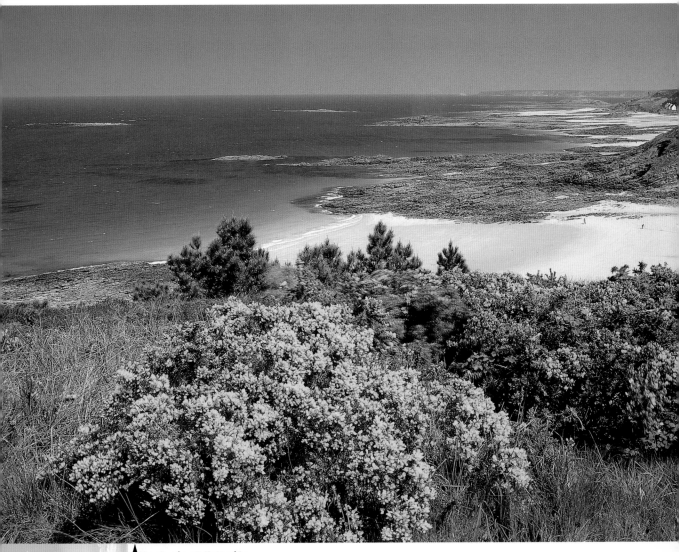

Technical Details

Medium-format SLR Camera with a 50mm wide-angle lens, 81C warm-up and polarising filters, and Fuji Velvia.

I used Fuji Velvia for this shot, taken on the Brittany coast of France, in order to maximise the rich colours of the yellow gorse and blue sea.

Rule of Thumb

When shooting on colour transparency film it is necessary to ensure you are using artificial-light film for indoor situations with tungsten lighting, as otherwise the pictures will have a pronounced orange cast. Conversely, this film will produce a strong blue cast if used in daylight.

Using Filters

Even in the best conditions, filters are often necessary, especially when shooting on transparency film. It's important to appreciate that colour transparency film is manufactured to give correct colour balance only in conditions when the light source is of a specific colour temperature. Daylight colour film is balanced to give accurate colours at around 5,600 degrees Kelvin but daylight can vary from only about 3,500 degrees K close to sundown, to nearly 20,000 degrees K in open shade when there is a blue sky.

The effect of an imbalance between the colour temperature of the light source and that for which the film is balanced can be very noticeable. The blue tint, for example, when shooting in open shade can be quite marked and in these situations a warm-up filter, such as an 81A or B is needed. In late afternoon the sunlight can be excessively warm for some subjects and then a blue-tinted filter such as an 82A or B is needed.

A polarising filter can be very useful for increasing the colour saturation of details such as foliage and for making the sky or sea a richer colour. It is equally effective when used with colour print film, whereas the qualities created by colour balancing filters can easily be achieved when making colour prints from negatives.

A polariser can also help to subdue excessively bright highlights when shooting into the light, like the sparkle on rippled water. Polarisers need between one and a half and two stops extra exposure but this will automatically be allowed for when using TTL metering.

I used a polarising filter for this seascape, taken in the Galicia region of Spain, to increase the colour saturation of the sky, make the clouds stand out in stronger relief and give the water a more translucent quality.

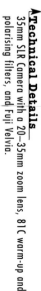

▲ Technical Details
35mm SLR Camera with a 20—35mm zoom lens, 81C warm-up and polarising filters, and Fuji Velvia.

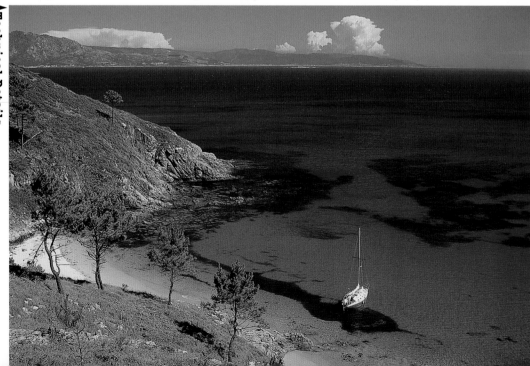

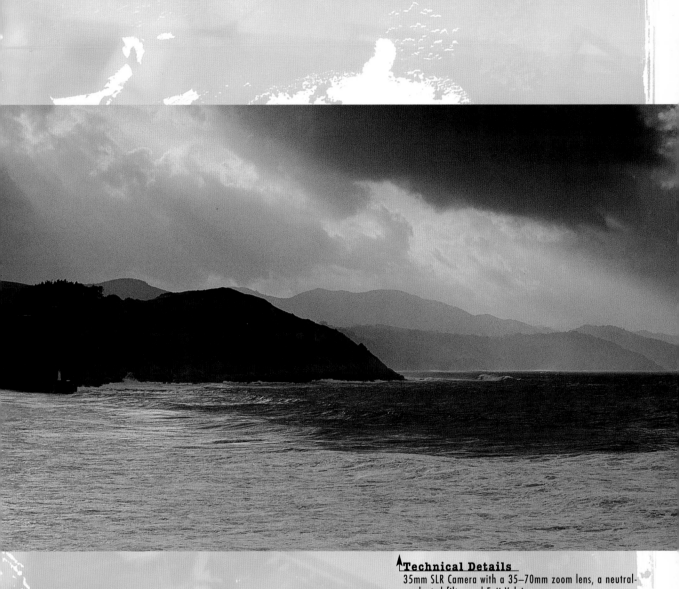

↑Technical Details

35mm SLR Camera with a 35–70mm zoom lens, a neutral-graduated filter and Fuji Velvia.

I used a neutral-graduated filter for this stormy seascape photographed on the north coast of Spain. It has prevented the sky from over-exposing, revealing richer tones and colour.

Neutral-graduated filters are a very effective means of making the sky darker and revealing richer tones and colours. They can also reduce the contrast between a bright sky and a darker foreground giving improved tones and colours in both. Coloured versions of these filters can also be bought but they do need to be used with discretion as the results can very easily look unnatural, and, unless used in the right circumstances, will tend to produce rather crude and obvious images.

Planning a Trip

The success of a photographic trip, even just a day out, depends a great deal upon planning and direction as it's important to have clear objectives and aims for the photographs you intend to take.

Technique

It's a good idea to write a list of the subjects you intend to photograph and, where possible, to mark the locations on a map with a highlight pen so that you have a rapid reference to the places you need to go.

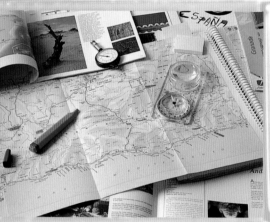

Technique

In addition to bookshops and libraries, regional and national tourist offices are often ideal sources of local information and a letter or fax to the public relations department can provide you with most of the things you need to know. Studying local postcards is also a helpful short cut to finding good subjects. As well as the important sites and places of interest it can be very useful to have a list of events such fairs and festivals as well as more everyday activities like markets.

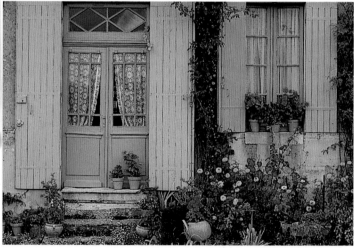

location
A village house near
Blaye - Gironde, France

This detail of shuttered windows and flowers, which I felt seemed to typify the French rural scene, helped to identify the location as well as being an attractive image.

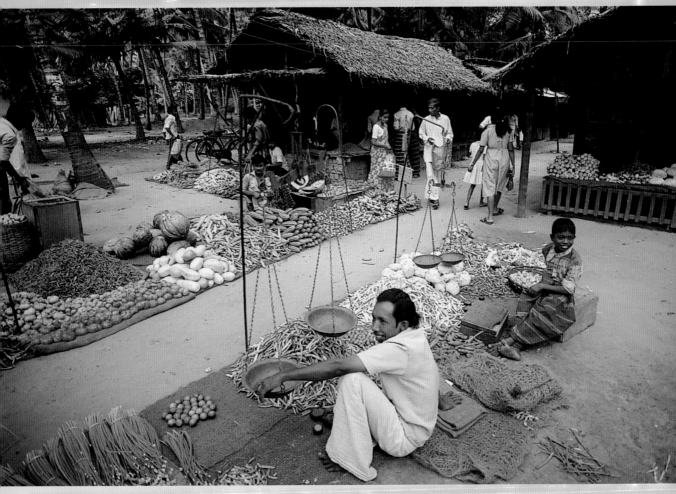

location
  A country market near Colombo - Sri Lanka
Local tourist information led me to this colourful village market.

Technical Details
  35mm Single Lens Reflex - 24mm lens,
  81B warm-up filter, Fuji Velvia.

Technical Details
  35mm Single Lens Reflex - 75-150mm zoom lens,
  81B warm-up filter, Fuji Velvia.

Travelling with a Camera

It's good to remember that, unless this is a holiday designed specifically to take photographs, it is wise to restrict the amount of equipment you take. Lugging a heavy camera bag around every day will very soon become a chore and the temptation to leave it behind "just today" will grow and grow.

I have what I call my minimalist kit which consists of a camera body, a set of filters, two zoom lenses and a converter which gives me a choice of focal lengths ranging from 24mm to 280mm and there are very few occasions when I really feel I need something else. However, I do carry a lightweight tripod which more than compensates for the effort by allowing me to shoot pictures in low light, such as night scenes, which would otherwise be impossible. A flash gun is useful on occasions when the light level is too low for available light photography and it can also be used for fill-in flash when shooting in contrasty sunlight, for example.

Customs

You can overcome many of the potential problems which might be experienced when passing through customs control if you make a duplicated list of all your equipment, together with serial numbers and keep it in your passport. This will also be invaluable if you have to make an insurance claim.

Insurance

It is best not to rely upon all-inclusive holiday insurance if you are carrying valuable cameras and lenses as they may well not be adequately covered. It is preferable to take out a specialist camera insurance and make sure it covers all the countries to which you are travelling.

I used a tripod for this interior photograph of an antique shop in New England, USA, as a slow shutter speed was needed to record the ambient light.

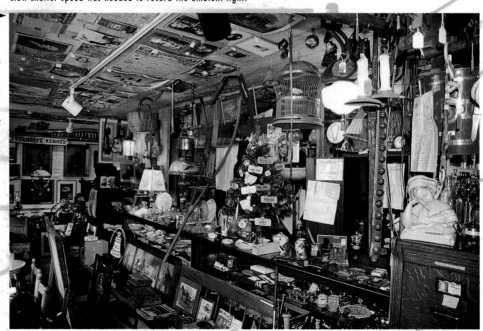

▲Technical Details
35mm SLR Camera with a 20–35mm zoom lens and Fuji Velvia.

Rule of Thumb

Make it a rule to never take a new and untried piece of camera kit away on a vacation. It is so much better to be really familiar with the equipment you are using; it will greatly reduce the risk of disappointments due to equipment failure if you stick to those which are tried and tested.

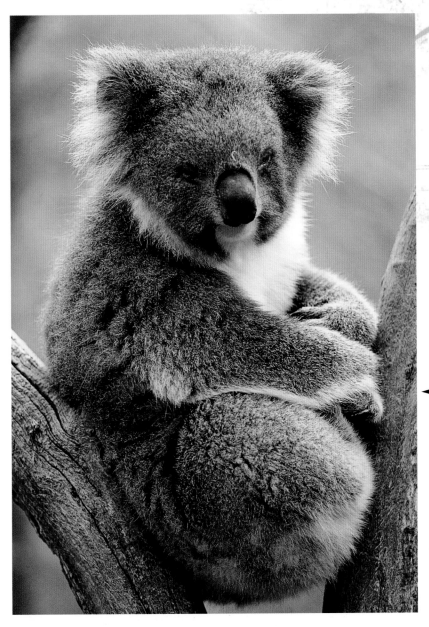

Technique

Carrying a quantity of film when travelling by air can be a problem these days as the **scanning equipment** used for luggage placed in the aircraft's hold can **seriously damage** film by fogging. It's now necessary to carry all your film as **hand luggage**. Unless it is very fast, in excess of ISO 1000, it will not come to any harm with the modern **X-ray machines** used in most international airports, but you can always try asking for a **hand search** if you are concerned.

I used a small flash gun to provide fill-in flash for this backlit shot of a Koala bear in order to enhance the texture of its fur.

◄ **Technical Details**
35mm SLR Camera with a 70–200mm zoom lens, an 81A warm-up filter and Fuji Velvia.

Rule of Thumb

It's wise to be well stocked with batteries as some types are difficult to find, especially if you are travelling off the beaten track. Also bear in mind that battery life is reduced in extremes of temperature.

Storing your Photographs

Card mounts are the most suitable way of storing and presenting colour transparencies. They can be printed with your name and address together with caption information using labels. Added protection can be given by the use of individual clear plastic sleeves which slip over the mount.

Technique

Even the finest print will be improved by good presentation, and mounting it flat onto a heavy-weight card is the first stage using dry-mounting tissue or spray adhesive. The addition of bevel cut-out mount on top will give it a very professional finish. You can cut these yourself to size using a craft knife – or there are special tools available – but they can also be bought ready-made in the most popular sizes from art stores. A group of prints finished in this way and nicely framed can look great on the walls of a home or office.

Technique

For purely personal use, many photographers use flip-over albums as a means of showing their prints. This method is, at best, simply a convenient way of storing prints and does nothing to enhance their presentation. It can be far more pleasing and effective to show a collection of images as a series of prints mounted on the pages of an album, choosing one large enough to allow six or more photos to be seen together on a spread.

There are a number of ways of selling your work and finding a potential outlet for it in print. Good colour photographs of all manner of subjects, ranging from landscapes to plants and gardens, architecture and people are in constant demand by publishers of magazines and there is a ready market for most topics if the photographs are well executed.

Rule of Thumb

Holiday experiences and accounts can be of considerable interest to a variety of magazines and if you have a collection of photographs on a particular destination, or of a certain hotel, restaurant or holiday activity, and can write, say, 1000 words to accompany them you will have an excellent chance of placing them with the right type of publication.

Rule of Thumb

The simplest way of storing mounted transparencies is in viewpacks – large plastic sleeves with individual pockets which can hold up to 24 35mm slides, or 15 of 120 transparencies. These can be fitted with bars for suspension in a filing-cabinet drawer and quickly and easily lifted out for viewing. For slide projection, however, it is far safer to use plastic mounts, preferably with glass covers, to avoid the risk of popping and jamming inside the projector.

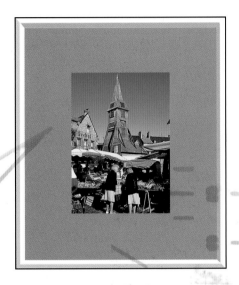

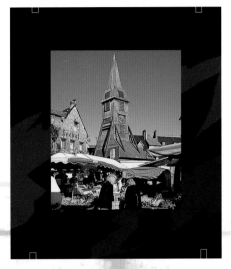

The different effects that can be created by changing the way a photographic print is mounted and presented are shown here.

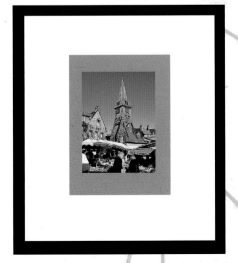

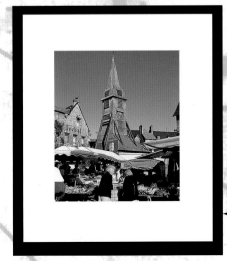

This shot, taken in a French country market, is the type of image regularly in demand by photo libraries and publishers as it can be used to illustrate a wide variety of very general topics such as lifestyle features and holidaying in France, for instance.

Technical Details

35mm SLR Camera with a 35–70mm zoom lens, an 81A warm-up filter and Fuji Velvia.

Technique

A slide show can be a very satisfying and enjoyable way of showing your photographs to family and friends with the advantage that they can all view them at the same time. You should edit your pictures carefully so that there are not too many similar images. It will also be more effective if you plan the sequence of slides in a way which creates variety; follow a photograph containing bright bold colours, for instance, with one which has a more subdued quality, a close-up with a view and a building with a landscape. This will ensure you retain your audience's attention and keep the presentation lively and interesting. A scripted commentary and even perhaps a soundtrack could make a slide show of an interesting vacation appreciated by a wider audience, such as at a camera club or other society.

Rule of Thumb

Look for ways in which you can vary the colour quality and composition of the images so that you are able to juxtapose them in the most effective way. Include both close-ups and long shots, wide-angle pictures with those more tightly framed and images which have different dominant colours. You are, effectively, designing a large image which is composed of many smaller ones, like tiles in a mosaic.

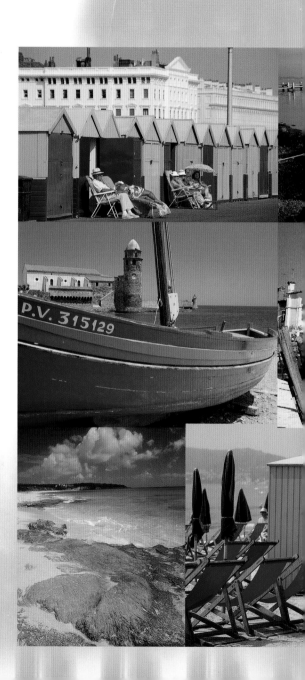

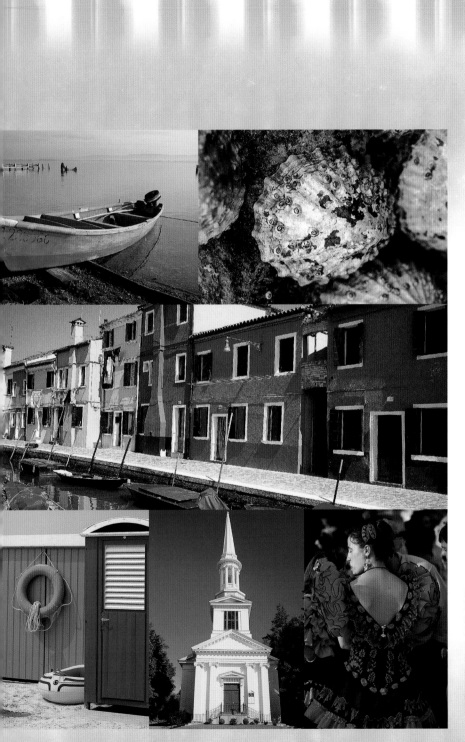

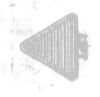

For a more permanent display, a pin board can make an effective and unusual addition to the decor of a kitchen, workroom or office. A large sheet of cork can be hung on a wall and a mosaic of prints fixed to it using either pins or some form of adhesive. Place the prints in a way which creates a pleasing juxtaposition varying both colours and subjects for maximum effect.

Selling your Work

There are a number of ways of finding a potential outlet for your work. The first is to exploit any other interests or expertise you might have. You may well buy, or read, magazines relating to other interests which have a travel context, such as golf, fishing, gardening, food and wine or walking for example. Good photographs of activities like these are in constant demand and there is a ready market for most subjects if the photographs are well executed.

Researching the Market

Spend some time in your local library, or at a friendly newsagents, and see just how the photographs are used in such publications and what type of image they seem to prefer. Make a note of some names, like the editor, features editor and picture editor.

The are some useful reference books available like the Freelance Writers and Artists Handbook and the Freelance Photographers Market Handbook, but these are, at best, only a general guide to potential users and it is vital to study each publication before you consider making a submission.

Think too about the pictures you have on your files in general, magazines represent only a tiny proportion of the publications which use photography. Travel brochures, for instance, are picture hungry and even fairly mundane shots like your holiday hotel or resort could be very welcome if it's well composed and has been shot under ideal conditions.

Illustrated Articles

While good individual photographs presented to the right publication stand a very good chance of being used there's no doubt that a complete package of words and photographs will stand a stronger chance. While the big glossy magazines will have well-known and regular writers, many smaller magazines have quite limited

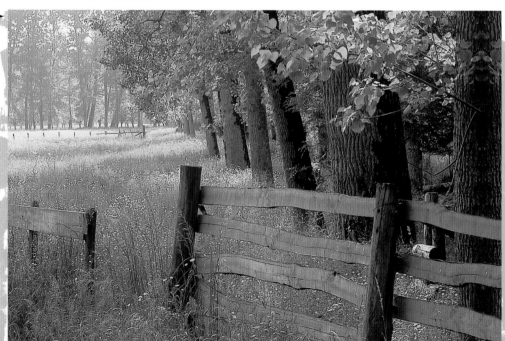

Technical Details
6x4.5cm Single Lens Reflex - 55-110mm zoom lens, 81C warm-up and polarising filters, Fuji Velvia.

location
The Marais Poitevin near Coulon - Deux Sevres, France

Generic images like these are often successful with the large international photolibraries as they are suitable for many purposes. This shot has sold countless times for uses ranging from magazine articles on the environment to air-conditioning brochures and tranquiliser advertisements.

resources and a clearly-written article of about a thousand words with a good selection of informatively-captioned photographs, illustrating the points made and the places described, will be a very tempting proposition.

Photo Libraries

A good photo library can reach infinitely more potential picture buyers than is possible for an individual and can also make sales to the advertising industry where the biggest reproduction fees are earned.

Making a Submission

As a general rule, you will be expected to submit several hundred transparencies initially, and will probably be obliged to allow those selected to be retained for a minimum period of three years. Your selection should be ruthlessly edited as only top-quality images will be considered and you should make sure that no very similar photographs are sent, only the very best of each situation.

Although a good photo library can produce a substantial income in time from a good collection of photographs it will take as much as a year before you can expect any returns and most libraries prefer photographers who make contributions on a fairly regular basis.

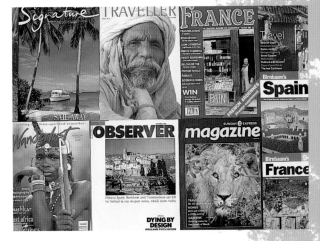

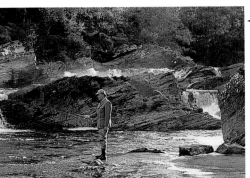

location
The River Oykel - Scotland

Technical Details
35mm Single Lens Reflex-
75-150mm zoom lens,
81C warm-up filter, Fuji Velvia.

A special knowledge or interest in a a topic like fishing, which is catered for by a large number of magazines and book publishers, can also produce images which have potential in a wide variety of other markets. This shot was used in a time-share brochure.

Glossary

Aperture Priority

An auto-exposure setting in which the user selects the aperture and the camera's exposure system sets the appropriate shutter speed.

APO Lens

A highly-corrected lens which is designed to give optimum definition at wide apertures and is most often available in the better quality long-focus lenses.

Ariel Perspective

The tendency of distant objects to appear bluer and lighter than close details, thereby enhancing the impression of depth and distance in an image.

Auto-bracketing

A facility available on many cameras which allows three or more exposures to be taken automatically in quick succession giving both more or less than the calculated exposure. Usually adjustable in increments of one third, half or one stop settings and especially useful when shooting colour transparency film.

Bellows Unit

An adjustable device which allows the lens to be extended from the camera body to focus at very close distances.

Black Reflector

A panel with a matt-black surface used to prevent light being reflected back into shadow areas in order to create a dramatic effect.

Cable Release

A flexible device which attaches to the camera's shutter release mechanism and which allows the shutter to be fired without touching the camera.

Close-up Lens

This is a weak positive lens placed in front of a prime lens to enable it to be focused at a closer distance than it is designed for. They can be obtained in various strengths and do not require an increase in exposure, as in the case of extension tubes and bellows units.

Colour Cast

A variation in a colour photograph from the true colour of a subject which is caused by the light source having a different colour temperature to that for which the film is balanced.

Colour Temperature

A means of expressing the specific colour quality of a light source in degrees Kelvin. Daylight colour film is balanced to give accurate colours at around 5,600 degrees Kelvin but daylight can vary from only 3,500 degrees K close to sundown to over 20,000 degrees K in open shade when there is a blue sky.

Cross-processing

The technique of processing colour transparency film in colour negative chemistry, and vice versa, to obtain unusual effects.

Data Back

A camera attachment which allows information like the time and date to be printed on the film alongside, or within the images.

Dedicated Flash
A flash gun which connects to the camera's metering system and controls the power of the flash to produce a correct exposure. Will also work when the flash is bounced or diffused.

Depth of Field
The distance in front and behind the point at which a lens is focused which will be rendered acceptably sharp. It increases when the aperture is made smaller and extends about two thirds behind the point of focus and one third in front. The depth of field becomes smaller when the lens is focused at close distances. A scale indicating depth of field for each aperture is marked on most lens mounts and it can also be judged visually on SLR cameras which have a depth of field preview button.

Double Extension
The term used when the lens is extended beyond the film plane to twice its focal length by the means of Macro focusing, Extension tubes or a Bellows unit to give a life-size image on the film. This requires four times the exposure indicated when the lens is focused at infinity, but will be automatically allowed for when using TTL (through-the-lens) metering.

DX Coding
A system whereby a 35mm camera reads the film speed from a bar code printed on the cassette and sets it automatically.

Evaluative Metering
An exposure-meter setting in which brightness levels are measured from various segments of the image and the results used to compute an average. It's designed to reduce the risk of under- or over-exposing subjects with an abnormal tonal range.

Exposure Compensation
A setting which can be used to give less or more exposure when using the camera's auto-exposure system for subjects which have an abnormal tonal range. Usually adjustable in one third of a stop increments.

Exposure Latitude
The ability of a film to produce an acceptable image when an incorrect exposure is given. Negative films have a significantly greater exposure latitude than transparency films.

Extension Tubes
Tubes of varying lengths which can be fitted between the camera body and lens to allow it to focus at close distances. Usually available in sets of three different widths.

Fill-in Flash
A camera setting, for use with dedicated flash guns, which controls the light output from a flash unit and allows it to be balanced with the subject's ambient lighting when it is too contrasty or there are deep shadows.

Filter Factor
The amount by which the exposure must be increased to allow for the use of a filter. A x2 filter requires an increase of one stop and a x4 filter requires a two stop exposure increase.

Flash Meter
An exposure meter which is designed to measure the light produced during the very brief burst from a flash unit.

Grey Card
A piece of card which is tinted to reflect 18% of the light falling upon it. It is the standard tone to which exposure meters are calibrated and can be used for substitute exposure readings when the subject is very light or dark in tone.

Honeycomb
A grill-like device which fits over the front of a light reflector to restrict its beam and limit spill.

Hyperfocal Distance
The closest distance at which details will be rendered sharp when the lens is focused on infinity. By focusing on the Hyperfocal distance you can make maximum use of the depth of field at a given aperture.

Incident Light Reading
A method – involving the use of a hand meter – of measuring the light falling upon a subject instead of that which is reflected from it.

ISO Rating
The standard by which film speeds are measured. Most films fall within the range of ISO 25 to ISO 3200. A film with double the ISO rating needs one stop less exposure and a film with half the ISO rating needs one stop more exposure. The rating is subdivided into one third of a stop settings i.e. 50, 64, 80, or 100.

Macro Lens
A lens which is designed to focus at close distances to produce up to a life-size image of a subject and is corrected to give its best performance at this range.

Matrix Metering
See Evaluative Metering.

Mirror Lock
A device which allows the mirror of an SLR camera to be flipped up before the exposure is made to reduce vibration and avoid loss of sharpness when shooting close-ups or using a long-focus lens.

Polarising Filter
A neutral grey filter which can reduce the brightness of reflections in non-metallic surfaces such as water, foliage and blue sky.

Programmed Exposure
An auto-exposure setting in which the camera's metering system sets both aperture and shutter speed according to the subject matter and lighting conditions. Usually offering choices like landscape, close-up, portrait, action etc.

Pulling
A means of lowering the stated speed of a film by reducing the development times.

Pushing
A means of increasing the stated speed of a film by increasing the development times.

Reciprocity Failure
The effect when very long exposures are given. Some films become effectively slower when exposures of more than one second are given and doubling the length of the exposure does not have as much effect as opening up the aperture by one stop.

Reversing Ring
A device which enables an ordinary lens to be mounted back to front on the camera, allowing it to be focused at very close distances and improving the definition.

Shutter Priority
A mode on auto-exposure cameras which allows the photographer to set the shutter speed while the camera's metering system selects the appropriate aperture.

Snoot
A conical device which fits over the front of a light reflector to restrict its beam and limit spill.

Spot Light
A light source fitted with a lens which enables a precisely focused beam of light to be projected.

Spot Metering
A means of measuring the exposure from a small and precise area of the image which is often an option with SLR cameras. It is useful when calculating the exposure from high-contrast subjects or those with an abnormal tonal range.

Substitute Reading
An exposure reading taken from an object of average tone which is illuminated in the same way as the subject. This is a useful way of calculating the exposure for a subject which is much lighter or darker than average.